Religious Origins of the Middle East Crisis, 2nd Edition

From Promise to Crisis to Solution

by

William J. Clark, Jr.

With

CH (COL) William J. Clark, Ret.

3rd in the *Keys To Understanding Life Series*

Religious Origins of the Middle East Crisis, 2nd Edition

Published by
William J. Clark, Jr.
with
CH (COL) William J. Clark, Ret.

3rd in the *Keys To Understanding Life Series*

www.KeysToUnderstandingLifeSeries.com
www.ReligiousOriginsMiddleEastCrisis.com

All Scripture taken from NEW AMERICAN STANDARD BIBLE®, Copyright © 1960, 1962, 1963, 1971, 1972, 1973, 1975, 1977, 1995 by The Lockman Foundation. Used by permission. All rights reserved.

Copyright © 2014 by William J. Clark, Jr.
All rights reserved.

No part of this publication may be reproduced, stored in a retrieval system or transmitted in any form or by any means electronic, mechanical, photocopying, recording or otherwise, without the prior written permission of the author.

ISBN 978-0-9900193-2-9

Cover and Artwork Design: Practical Photography & Publishing

Printed in the United States of America
U.S. Printing History
First Edition: July 2012
Second Edition: October 2014

Table of Contents

CHAPTER 1: PROMISE TO CRISIS 1
  The Bottom Line 1
  What You'll Find In This Book 2
  Other Goals Of This Book 3
  God According To Jews, Christians and Muslims 4
  Jewish, Christian And Muslim Scriptures 7
  Abraham , a.k.a. Abram (c. 2000 B. C.) 8
    The Middle Eastern Connection to God 8
    God Makes Promises to Abraham 9
    Understanding the Middle East Crisis Involves
      Understanding the Spiritual Dimension, Not Just
      the Religious Differences 14
    Key Spiritual Battle: Sarai To Trust God's
      Promises and Direction through Abram 16
  **Failing Key Trials Leads To The Beginnings of Two
    Middle Eastern Religions** 18
    Key Spiritual Battle: Whether Abram and Sarai
      Should Follow Cultural Custom 19
    Key Spiritual Battle: Abraham to Go Against
      Cultural Custom 20
    Other Information About Ishmael and His Line 24
    Key Spiritual Battle: Jacob's Favoritism Toward
      Joseph 25
    Key Spiritual Battle: The Trial of Israel in Slavery
      and of Those in the Promised Land 27
  Israel's Exodus From Egypt (c. 1450 B. C.) 30
    Key Spiritual Battle: Pharaoh's Economic and
      National Security Trial 31
    Israel After Slavery 36
  Jonah's Trial (782 B. C.) 37
    Key Spiritual Battle: Jonah Not Wanting To
      Minister To the Lost 37
    Israel After Jonah 39
  Israel Under The Romans (63 B.C.) 40
  Jesus The Messiah (33 A. D.) 40

    Key Spiritual Battle: Accepting Jesus as the
        Messiah 40
    Jewish Views of the Messiah 42
Israel Dispersed (70 A. D.) 44
    Key Spiritual Battle: Israel Conquered and
        Dispersed 45
Palestine Is Created (66 - c. 135 A. D.) 46
Christianity Before Islam (300 A. D. – 634 A. D.) 46
    The Authenticity of the Christian Bible 47
Muhammad And The Birth Of Islam (610 A. D.) 51
Muslim Civil War (650 A. D.) 53
Druze And The Shiite Controversy (1017 A. D.) 54
Christianity After 1054 A. D. 57
    Key Spiritual Battle: Convert, Leave, or Die 58
    Christians Relate to Jews in Light of Old Testament
        Israel 60
Israel Is Restored (1948) 61
Israel Today (1948 - present) 61

CHAPTER 2: THE PRESENT SITUATION 65
Scope 65
Differences In Problem-Solving 65
    Overview of Challenges for Non-Muslim
        Politicians 66
    Problems for Christian Politicians 66
    The Illusion of Muslim Political Leaders 67
    Problems in Believing a Muslim Leader's Word 68
    The Challenge of Recognizing A Muslim Leader's
        Intentions 69
    A Christian Perspective on These Problems 71
    Perspectives on Christian Religious Roots 72
**More About How Muslims, Christians And Jews
Relate 75**
    Tolerance Between Jews, Christians and Muslims 75
    Why "Good Muslims" Don't Take Care of
        Changing the "Bad Muslims" 76

CHAPTER 3: CRISIS TO SOLUTION 79
**The Middle East Crisis Is Similar To Everyone's
Spiritual Crises 79**
Misperceptions Of God And Ourselves Fuel Crisis 81

What Happens When We Are Wrong? 83
How Does God Seek To Communicate Solutions To Every Person? 83
MYTHS About Hearing/Embracing God's Solutions 84
Hearing/Discerning God's Solutions (Christian Perspective) 88
Possible Solutions 91
    The Holy Spirit's Role in Resolving any Conflict or Crisis...93
    Challenges for Christians And Solution 3 95
    A Final Consideration 98

APPENDIX 1: RELIGIOUS COMPOSITION OF NATIONS ...99
APPENDIX 2: DEFINITIONS **101**
APPENDIX 3: REFERENCES **117**
APPENDIX 4: LIST OF FIGURES **121**
OTHER TITLES IN THE KEYS TO UNDERSTANDING LIFE SERIES **122**
ABOUT THE AUTHORS..**124**

Chapter 1: Promise To Crisis

The Bottom Line

Israel became a modern nation in 1948, after World War II. Many people think that this was the beginning of the Middle East crisis. This view causes us to think that the crisis, and any possible solution, deals with politics and diplomacy among nations. However, the conflict is much more than politics and diplomacy. In truth, the crisis goes back to one man – the biological and religious father of the Jew, the Muslim, and, believe it or not, the Christian!

As distasteful as it may be to us in the West, the truth is that behind all the concern about the children, the broken families and the costs of war, the crisis actually deals with differences in religious beliefs. But, don't let that scare you. Whether you hold to any particular religious beliefs or not, if you want to understand the crisis between the peoples of the Middle East, you have to understand what drives them. This means certain basics of the Jews, Christians and Muslim beliefs must be understood.

While this book will inform you on some key historical events pertaining to today's crisis, it is important to realize that the history isn't simply a back story to the Middle East. The history of the Middle East peoples, as well as their conduct today, is about their religious beliefs. For many in the Middle East, their identity as individuals is about living a religious legacy that their history provides.

The goal of this book is to help you understand the importance of the religious identity of the people of the Middle East. It will help you understand the differences of the religions that arose from the Middle East. Together, these will help you understand that, in the end, diplomacy, humanitarian concerns, military interventions and politics will always be limited to short-term solutions.

Chapter 1: Promise To Crisis

WHAT YOU'LL FIND IN THIS BOOK

1. **Definitions:** This feature of the book clarifies a number of words, abbreviations, etc. that we hear or see in the news, which aren't always explained in the news. The first time we mention one of these in the text, you will see it in all CAPS. If you want a simple definition, flip back to Appendix 2 (page 101) and look it up. We'll remind you about this for the first few times that words in all CAPS appear, just in case you forget this is available to you.

2. **Key Spiritual Battles:** This feature points to a few key historical and religious figures you need to know about. These people made decisions that led to or fueled the conflict all the way up to today. These are presented from a Christian perspective. As such, these point out how a person's success or failure in discerning God's guidance impacts not only that person's life, but the lives of others as well!

3. **Chapter 1:** This chapter lays out how things got the way they are in the Middle East, and why the conflict actually revolves around religious beliefs.

4. **Chapter 2:** This chapter builds on Chapter 1 and highlights a couple key differences in how Middle Eastern peoples relate with one another, and with those of us in the West. It explains why Western political strategies and approaches can't create long-term solutions.

5. **Chapter 3:** This chapter specifically focuses on key questions and issues (from the authors' view) that persons of faith can consider when determining how well they are living for God.

We (the authors) have attempted to be as objective as possible concerning the major religions of the Middle East, including an overview of what they believe and how it relates to what we see happening in the Middle East today. However, there are some portions of the book that are viewed from a primarily Christian perspective – particularly in Chapter 3. We will point these out.

OTHER GOALS OF THIS BOOK

The religious identity of the peoples in the Middle East isn't the only important point to get from this book. As we go along, you will want to pay attention to the four additional points below. If you are a Christian, you will be able to see how these points are directly related to how well we, as Christians, represent the Lord.

If you aren't a person of faith, we hope these points will help you see why the Bible and the Christian faith challenge Christians to stand strongly for God in ways that are often different from the world, even when it goes against various Western values. The points below are expressed from a Christian perspective. Jews and Muslims have different perspectives and interpretations about these points.

1. **All mankind experiences trials**. Trials can include any form of life difficulty or decision. Behind all trials are spiritual battles involving whether we will live dependently on God and overcome evil's temptations and deceptions (1 Corinthians 10:13). Trials are part of the larger spiritual war between Satan and God. In every trial, Satan seeks to influence a person's decision-making, while God seeks to grow, change, and bring the person closer to Him through the trial (Hebrews 12:7-11).

2. **There is a spiritual war behind the human events that have unfolded in the Middle East**. Our own "trials and tribulations" are spiritual battles we face because we too are part the spiritual war (Ephesians 6:10-12).

3. **God loves everyone**. This includes both believer and non-believer. This doesn't mean that God is OK with everyone's actions. God's love is always demonstrated in the many trials (spiritual battles) a person faces, whether that person is able to discern and/or feel loved by God in his trials. God tries to reach out to both believer and non-believer, in order to guide and lead each of us to Himself. He does this because He loves us (John 3:16).

4. **"Passing" a particular trial so God lives through us requires discernment on our part**. Discernment involves

Chapter 1: Promise To Crisis

identifying what God wants us to change in us during a trial. It involves inclining our heart to Him and embracing that change during the trial. Discernment deals with figuring out how to get to a place of peace during a trial (John 14:27; Colossians 3:15), and how to submit to God's lead in responding to the trial (Hebrews 5:11-14).

In addition helping you understand the religious history behind the Middle East crisis, one of the authors' goals is to point to the importance of discernment to the Christian walk. This is emphasized in the *Key Spiritual Battles* feature of the book, and in Chapter 3. The goal is to encourage believers to examine themselves, in terms of how well they are able to discern God's guidance to them in trials. Another goal is to encourage believers to support the strengthening of those in the Body, who claim to follow Christ, yet who struggle to make sense of their trials and life difficulties. So, if you are a Christian, when you come to one of the *Key Spiritual Battles* features discussed in the book, ask yourself whether you can discern God's guidance in any trial you face. If you feel you, or others you know, need more training in the area of discernment, check out the other titles offered by the authors at the back of this book.

GOD ACCORDING TO JEWS, CHRISTIANS AND MUSLIMS

Remember, words in all CAPS are further explained
in Appendix 2, starting on page 101.

To begin, we need to clarify a common misconception regarding God. In this book, when we talk about God, we mean the God of Abraham, Isaac and Jacob.

One thing the JEWS, the CHRISTIANS and the MUSLIMS have in common is that they believe there is only one God. The one God that they all believe exists is the God of Abraham. However the Jews, Christians and Muslims have different views of what kind of God He is, what kind of character God has, and on what God has said, has done, is doing and will do. Be patient as we clarify what this actually means.

The Christians believe that God, the God of Abraham, Isaac and Jacob sent His only Son to earth to die for our sins. Christians believe JESUS (see MESSAGE OF CHRIST in definitions starting on page 101 for more information) is God's Son. While the Jews and Muslims agree that Jesus existed, the Jews and Muslims do not agree with Christians that Jesus was the Son of God.

There are many Old Testament, Hebrew names that the Jews have for God. Many of these names reflect their view of God's character. Some names are like "titles" for God. Christians can embrace these Hebrew names for God. The Jews have many names for God in Hebrew; the Muslims have one name for God. It is a title. In English, it's "The God." In Arabic, ALLAH is how you say "God," or "The God."

There are two key reasons why Christians often mistakenly think that Allah is a reference to a completely different "god" than that of the God of Abraham, Isaac and Jacob.
1. The first reason is because the Muslims have such a sharply different perspective of God, His character and His will. It is difficult for Christians to understand that Muslims are, in fact, referring to the God of Abraham when they talk about their beliefs.
2. The second reason is because non-Arabic Muslims will almost always refer to God in Arabic. For example, a German Muslim will not refer to God in his native tongue, which would be "Gott." Instead, a German Muslim will likely refer to God in Arabic, saying, "Allah." This is true whether the non-Arabic Muslim is American, German, French, Russian, or whatever nationality. Naturally, when a Christian hears an American Muslim refer to Allah, it can come across as if Allah is a reference to a "god" other than the God of Abraham, Isaac and Jacob.

While we will touch on this again, there are specific reasons why a Muslim is almost required to speak God's name in Arabic. One reason is because Arabic is the language in which Muhammad claimed the God of Abraham, Isaac and Jacob spoke to him. Another reason is

Chapter 1: Promise To Crisis

because in Islam, the QUR'AN is only to be spoken in Arabic. In Islam, a good Muslim, even one who is not Arabic, is expected to learn enough Arabic to recite portions of the Qur'an, and perhaps even to say some prayers in Arabic. In fact, many Muslims prohibit the translation of the Qur'an into any other language (although it has been done extensively – you can even access copies of the Qur'an as a reference online)!

Many Muslims would take offense if a non-Muslim even possessed a copy of the Qur'an, let alone in a language other than Arabic. Finally, it is not unheard of for Muslims in primarily Muslim nations to attempt to pass laws prohibiting non-Muslims from speaking the name of God in Arabic, i.e., to prohibit non-Muslims from saying, "Allah." For these reasons, it is not surprising that Christians sometimes mistakenly think that Allah is referring to a "god" other than the God of Abraham, Isaac and Jacob, or other than the same God, Whom the Christians believe sent His Son Jesus to die on the cross.

As we progress and get to the section on Muhammad and the birth of Islam (page 51), you will read more about why the Muslims say that their God is the God of Abraham, Isaac and Jacob, but they are more likely to refer to God as the God of Abraham, Ishmael and Muhammad. It is still the same God to which they refer, but, as we mentioned already, the Jews, Christians and Muslims have some *very* different views of what kind of God He is, what kind of character God has, and on what God has said, has done, is doing and will do.

One last point, you will find only a few places in this book where we use the Arabic title, "Allah." In most cases we will simply say God. We might express things like, "The Muslims claim that God...," or "From the Muslim view, God...," etc. We (authors) have one purpose for this: to help you, the reader, to remember that while your personal beliefs may differ from any of the faith groups we speak about here, when the Muslims speak of "Allah," they are talking about their view of the God of the Jews and the Christians. It is important, particularly for Christians, that we are not so carried away by the emotions which can arise from being offended by the Muslim view, that we are unable to correctly understand the view itself. This isn't going to fix the Middle East crisis; however, if we can't correctly verbalize the differences and similarities we have with others, then we will foster confusion amongst the Body of Christ. As Christians, we don't need to foster confusion within the Body of Christ.

JEWISH, CHRISTIAN AND MUSLIM SCRIPTURES

The Jews, the Christians and the Muslims each has Scriptures that they believe come from God. Below are the Scriptures according to each of these religious faiths.

1. **The Jews have the TANAKH, the Hebrew Bible**. (Remember, the words in all CAPS are further explained in Appendix 2, starting on page 101.) While it is divided differently from the Christian Bible, contents of the Tanakh are mostly similar. The Tanakh consists of three parts: Torah (sometimes called the Five Books of Moses), Nevi'im (the books of the Jewish Prophets), and Ketuvim (or "Writings").

2. **The Christians have The Holy BIBLE**. The Bible has two parts: the Old Testament and the New Testament. Each of these is made of "books" and/or "letters." Some Christian denominations have a couple more or a couple fewer books in their version of the Bible, but the majority is basically the same. The Old Testament essentially is the same as the Hebrew Bible.

3. **The Muslims have the QUR'AN**. The Qur'an contains messages or revelations, which MUHAMMAD claimed that God (the God of Abraham) gave to him. There are some similarities between the Qur'an, the Hebrew Bible and the Christian Bible. Qur'an 3.3 mentions the Torah, which is the first five books of the Hebrew and Christian Bibles. The Qur'an also refers to the Gospels (first books in the Christian Bible's New Testament). The Qur'an talks about Adam (as in Adam and Eve), Noah, Moses, David, JONAH, King Solomon, John the Baptist, Mary, JESUS (MESSAGE OF CHRIST), and others, who are also mentioned in the Hebrew and Christian Bibles. (Remember, words in all CAPS are further explained in

Chapter 1: Promise To Crisis

Appendix 2, starting on page 101.) However, some of the accounts in the Qur'an are different from the Hebrew and Christian Bibles. Some of the stories are similar, but have different endings to those stories. Muslims embrace the similarities and differences with the Tanakh and The Bible *as presented in the Qur'an*.

To understand the conflict in the Middle East, it is important to grasp the Muslim point of view of the Tanakh and the Bible. The Muslim view is that the existing versions of the Bible and Tanakh are corrupted and inaccurate. This is one reason why Muslims believe that God gave the Qur'an to Muhammad as the "Final Testament" of uncorrupted truth. So while todays Bible and Tanakh have some truth in them with which the Muslims agree, according to ISLAM, the Qur'an's versions of the stories are the uncorrupted, final and corrected versions from God.

ABRAHAM, A.K.A. ABRAM (C. 2000 B. C.)

Abraham is central to the people of the Middle East, to their feelings of the legitimacy and to the power of their beliefs. In this section we will look at three PROMISES that the Jew, the Christian and the Muslim believe God made to Abraham. We will also look at some Key Spiritual Battles in which he made certain decisions in response to his understanding of these promises from God.

The Middle Eastern Connection to God

One of the key persons mentioned in all three religions' Scriptures is ABRAM. This man's name later changed to Abraham. The Tanakh and Bible say that God changed his name (Genesis 17:5). Abraham's wife was Sarai; God changed her name to Sarah.

The changing of their names was not just a cultural thing. It wasn't like having a nickname. It was deeply significant because it reflected the idea that their identity was literally altered in light of their growing relationship with God! The Jew, the Christian and the Muslim viewed Abraham and Sarah as literally transformed by God. The name change reflected an agreement that they believe the Creator of the Universe made with the man, Abraham.

The power of one's transformation by God is reflected in the changing of names of other persons in the Tanakh and the Christian Bible. The power of this transformation is carried into today by the traditions of baptism for the Christians and somewhat in the bar mitzvah for the Jews. As far as the Muslims go, there is no one particular act or event that reflects the transformation of a person into a good Muslim. Generally speaking, for the Muslims, the more one adheres to the FIVE PILLARS OF FAITH, the more one tends to be viewed as or feel like a good Muslim.

Back to Abraham. Abraham was born in what is now modern day Iraq, in what was then known as Ur of the Chaldees (see Figures 1.1 and 1.2 on the following pages). After marrying Sarah, Abraham joined his father and other extended family as they traveled about 700 miles to a place called Haran. Haran lies along what is today an area on the border of Turkey and Syria.

God Makes Promises to Abraham

Genesis 12:1-8 records that while in Haran, Abraham received three promises from God. The Jews, the Christians and the Muslims agree that Abraham was about 75 years old and that God made these promises to him.*

---

* The first promise is mentioned in the Qur'an (2.124). While the other two are not directly mentioned in the Qur'an, the Muslims still believe God made the promises. The Muslims agree with each of the promises, but their view is that the fulfillment of them passed from Abraham through Ishmael to Muhammad. Muslims would claim that the second promise of blessing the world was fulfilled in Muhammad himself, and that the third promise of land was fulfilled shortly after Muhammad's death, but was violated with the re-establishment of the State of Israel in 1948.

Chapter 1: Promise To Crisis

1. **Promise 1** (Genesis 12:2): "I will make you a great Nation." This promise holds the belief of a personal blessing to Abraham.
2. **Promise 2** (Genesis 12:3): "In you, all families...will be blessed." This promise holds the belief of a universal blessing through Abraham to others.
3. **Promise 3** (Genesis 12:1 and 7): "To your descendants I will give this land." This promise holds the belief of a national blessing, i.e., a blessing for the nation of people God promised in His first promise.

God promised certain land to Abraham for his descendants. This became known as the "Promised Land" to the Jews and Christians. This is the land that is in dispute today between the Palestinians (see PALESTINE) and various Muslim groups, who want ISRAEL to cease to exist. While the Palestinians, Israelis, etc. may say a reason for fighting is to fight for their right to exist as a people, underneath that is their belief in the legitimacy of their right to fulfill the third promise God made to Abraham.

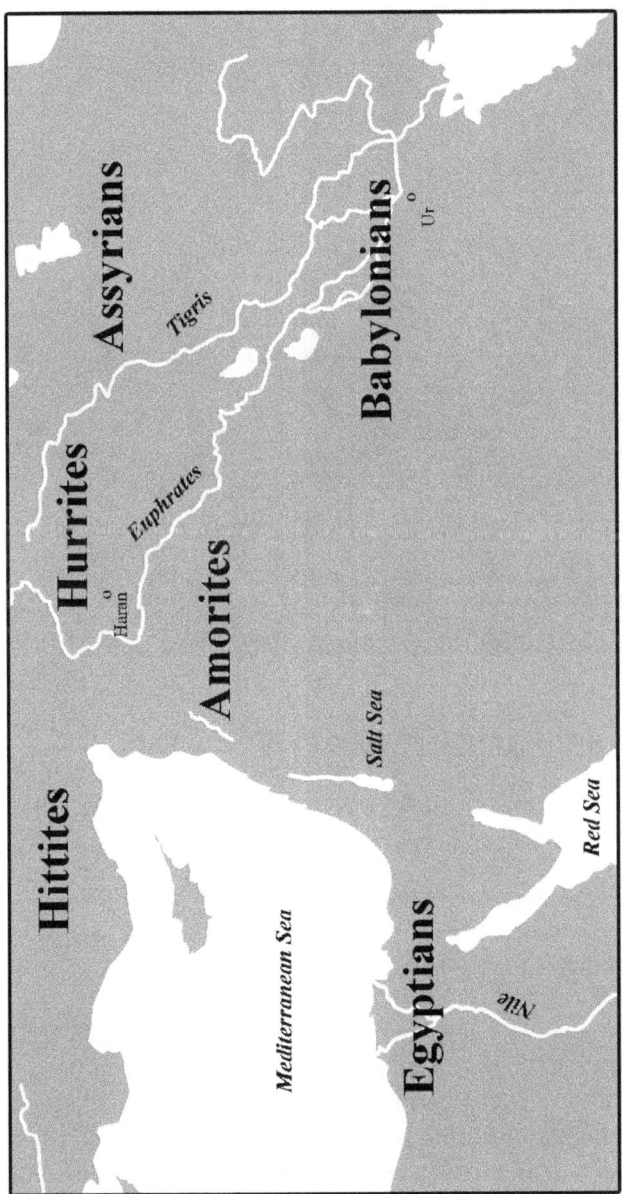

Figure 1.1 – Who Was Where At Time Of The Promises

Figure 1.1 shows the main groups of people and their locations around 2000 B.C. when God made the three promises to Abraham. The Promised Land itself was occupied by smaller tribes and peoples. This figure also shows the approximate locations of Ur and Haran.

Chapter 1: Promise To Crisis

Photo taken by SGT William Witcher (RET).

Figure 1.2 – Abraham's House In Ur

Figure 1.2 shows a photo taken in 2009 of some restored ruins believed to be Abraham's house or birthplace in Ur. The site was discovered by British archeologists in the 1930s. Supposedly, in 1999, Saddam Hussein had the house restored from its original foundation, which was all that was remaining. The site is a protected archeological dig site today. Note that the land is very dry and barren. In Abraham's day, this area was lush and fertile.

The boundaries of the Promised Land are outlined in both the Tanakh and the Bible. The boundary descriptions include lands formerly belonging to many ancient tribes of people, from the River of Egypt to the Euphrates River. However, today we really don't know where some of the people mentioned in those verses were actually located. Several of those tribes of people have been lost to history.

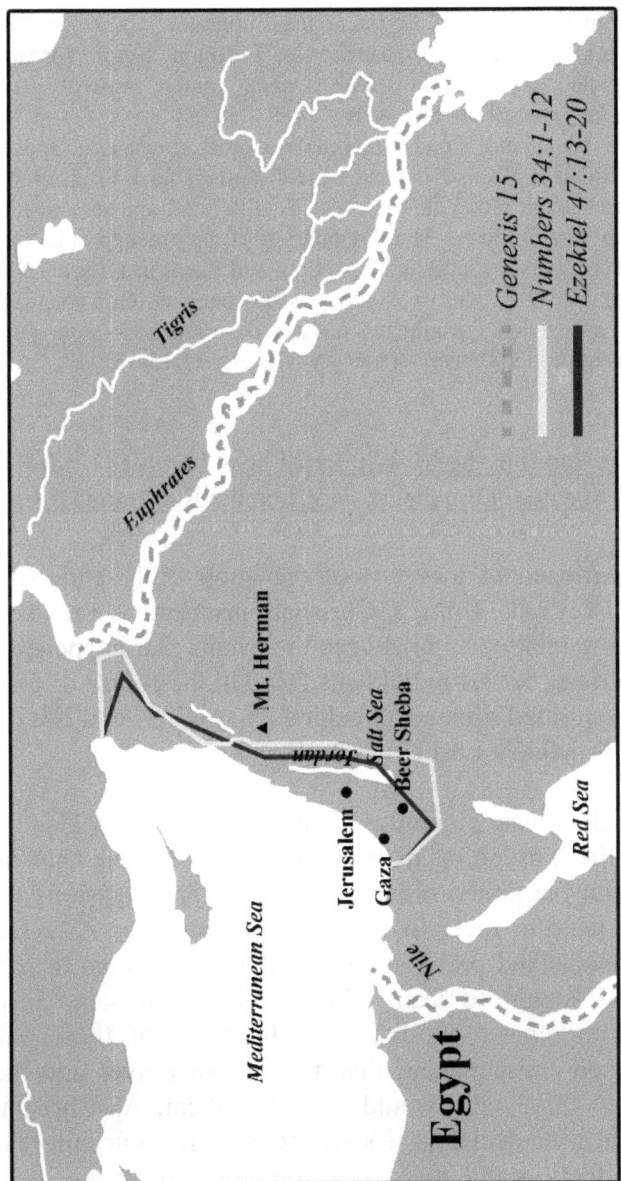

Figure 1.3 – Biblical Descriptions Of The Promised Land

This figure shows three geographical areas describing the extent of the Promised Land.
1. The boundaries of the first, found in Genesis 15:18-21, is in red above. This description seems to define the Promised Land. It is a large area,

Chapter 1: Promise To Crisis

"from the brook of Egypt to the Euphrates." It would include all of Israel, the Palestinian Territories, Lebanon, Syria, Jordan, and Iraq, Kuwait, Saudi Arabia, U.A.E, Oman, Yemen, most of Turkey, and all the land east of the Nile river.

2. The Bible and Tanakh record two other times God spoke about the boundaries of the Promised Land (Numbers 34:1-12; Ezekiel 47:13-20). These areas much smaller than the first, and are only somewhat larger than Israel today. The boundaries of the second and third Biblical descriptions are outlined in yellow and black in Figure 1.3. While God promised this land to Abraham's descendants, God told Abraham that his descendants would not possess the Promised Land until after they had been in 400 years of slavery (Genesis 15:13-14).

Understanding the Middle East Crisis Involves Understanding the Spiritual Dimension, Not Just the Religious Differences

As we mentioned at the start of the book, fully understanding the Middle East Crisis from a Christian perspective requires that we recognize the relationship between the events that happened in history and the spiritual battles individuals faced in the course of those events. This is the spiritual dimension behind all conflicts and life difficulties, including the Middle East Crisis itself.

While Abraham was given three great promises from God, that didn't mean his life was going to be easy. It didn't mean that he'd never struggle with the kinds of questions, issues and decisions with which all people have to face. In fact, Abraham and his wife faced many major decisions and problems which challenged them to respond and act as God sought to lead. Abraham failed in some respects and succeeded in others, so did his wife. Each of their failures and successes had consequences that affected their lives and the lives of others, even those who would live after them. As Christians today, when we face life decisions, issues and concerns, our failure or success similarly affects us and others.

The Bible, the Tanakh and the Qur'an each contain many stories of persons who faced struggles and concerns. It is in these times that a person is challenged to overcome evil's deceptions and temptations in order to live for God. In the Christian world, these kinds of life issues are known as trials, or spiritual battles.

Trials are situations that, when we experience them, usually cause us to want to figure out a solution that leads to the best outcome. Trials involve making a decision. In trial situations, not making a decision is actually a decision.

The Christian Bible highlights at least two reasons why trials are tough. First, they are tough because we want to be able to influence how the situation turns out, i.e., we want the trial to turn out the way we think it should turn out (this principle is reflected in many of the trials we read in the Bible, for example Ananias and Sapphira – Acts 5:1-10, those of Peter – Matthew 14:22-33; 16:21-23; 26:33-35, 36-45, 50-54, 69-75; John 13:5-11; Galatians 2:11-14, etc.). Second, trials are tough because there are spiritual issues behind the external situation (this principle is reflected in the Book of Job, specifically Job 1:1-12).

Many times we are not really fully able to put our finger on the spiritual aspects of a trial. Still, we can learn how to see and verbalize these spiritual aspects more skillfully, and how to respond to them as God would have us to respond. Doing so involves DISCERNMENT.

Discernment is critical to letting God live through us during trials. When we improperly discern the spiritual dimensions of a trial, we will not be aware of Satan's deception in the trial (James 1:13-15). In fact, without discernment we will usually fall to the deception, sometimes without even realizing we've gone against God's will. This is why Satan is often called, "The Deceiver." Jesus pointed out that even while keeping "the letter of the LAW," we sin when we miss the spirit of God's tenants, commands and guidelines (Matthew 12:1-14) that are applicable to the trial we face.

Behind all the historical events, which have collectively led to what we call "The Middle East Crisis," are trials. As we go along, we will look at some of these trials, as well as a couple situations that likely presented the historical person with a trial. There is not enough room to do this with all the trials throughout history. But of the ones we look at, each brings out lessons that can help us see how important it is to accurately discern the guidance God offers to us for responding to our trials. With that in mind, let's start by looking at a likely trial situation for both Abram and his wife Sarai – before God changed their names.

Chapter 1: Promise To Crisis

Key Spiritual Battle: Sarai To Trust God's Promises and Direction through Abram

The Bible does not say that Sarai experienced a trial once God gave Abram the three promises and then went to tell her about them. However, were we in Sarai's position, we can see it is not unlikely that we might experience a trial. With this in mind, let's see how this very well could have been one of the first key spiritual battles that ultimately lead to the Middle East Crisis.

Trial Overview (Genesis 12:1-8): Abram and Sarai had to trust God by moving from Haran without knowing where they were going.
1. Concerning God's first promise of a great nation, Sarai was barren and unable to have children (Genesis 11:30). Abram and Sarai had to trust that somehow God would work things out to create a great nation from them.
2. Concerning God's second promise, that the world would be blessed through Abram, he and Sarai also had to trust God. The details in how this promise would be fulfilled were not stated by God.
3. Concerning God's third promise of land, they would have to trust God because the land was inhabited by others. Additionally, God told Abram that the land would go to Abram's descendants, not necessarily to Abram and Sarai (Genesis 12:7).
4. Abram and Sarai ended up walking about 400 miles before God alerted them that they had arrived in the Promised Land.
5. When they arrived in the Promised Land, there was a famine. They had to go down to Egypt, which involved walking another 400 miles. Of course, later it would involve yet another 400 miles on their return trip from Egypt!

Reality Check: Again, the Bible does not specifically say that Sarai experienced a trial when Abram went home one day and told her about the promises God made to him. But, imagine being Sarai. While Abram had an "experience" with God, the Bible does not say the same about Sarai. The implication is that she had to take Abram's word about the promises! Again, Sarai was barren, so having a child would literally involve a miracle. Sarai was going to have to trust that Abram's understanding of what God said was true.

Another challenge that Sarai possibly faced was that she was going to have to move away from family. Though she was barren and could not have her own children, it might have been of some comfort to her that she was able to live with the rest of the family in Haran, along with their children. Perhaps you can see that trusting in God's promises as stated by Abram could have challenged Sarai to give up what comfort she received from living with the extended family in Haran (although Lot and his family would end up moving with Abram and Sarai). Trusting in God's promises meant that Sarai would have to be willing to move without knowing where they were going. If any of us found ourselves in a similar situation, we would likely experience any of these things as a trial.

Any of these issues for Sarai could have been significant enough to cause her to be tempted to resist Abram. Satan uses normal desires and concerns like these to deceive us into fighting and experiencing marital strife. If Sarai did not discern how God would have her respond to Abram, her resistance could have in turn tempted Abram to question that he received the promises or understood them correctly!

Discernment Challenge: Discerning When, Who, And How To Trust. A big part of what we sometimes must discern and accept in trials, as far as following God's will, is that it is not always going to be easy or comfortable for us, even though God loves us and is trying to grow us in a trial. Were we in Sarai's shoes, would we trust in both God and Abram so fully with our hearts that we would be looking forward to the move? Or, would we grumble about our doubts the entire trip? Were we Sarai, would we "put our foot down" and insist that we not move until we at least know where we are going and are sure that that place would be better than living where we are? As Sarai, would we have a glad heart in moving even though we could not corroborate any of the promises that God made and even though there was no sign or proof to her that God even made them? These issues and concerns were all part of the challenge for Sarai in discerning that God wanted her to trust Him and Abram.

Chapter 1: Promise To Crisis

Trial Outcome: Abram and Sarai did exhibit trust towards God in that they moved. In this way, they "passed the test." While this took a great amount of discernment and faith on both Sarai and Abram's parts, their hearts were strong with God and they would be blessed for this.

As we mentioned, when God finally told Abram that they arrived in the Promised Land, there was a famine in it (Genesis 12:10)! How would that potentially affect your husband/wife relationship were you in that trial? If you were in Sarai's position, would this rekindle any doubts you had? Would you be able to discern God's guidance and remain strong in it if the place God sent you had a famine in it?

One thing the Bible shows us is that just because we make it through one spiritual battle does not mean we won't have any more spiritual battles. We see this with Abram and Sarai when they walk into a famine-ridden land! This very well could have introduced another trial, or spiritual battle. The Bible doesn't go into how things went between Abram and Sarai concerning the famine, but the point is that we too often experience obstacles in our own life events. They can cause us to doubt what we once understood to be God's direction for us. The Tanakh and Christian Bible indicate that Abram did "stay the course" God set for him... for the most part. Abram often discerned God's guidance to him and when he did, Abram placed his faith in God.

Abram and Sarai continued on to Egypt where there was food. This opened them up to other significant spiritual battles and trials. While in Egypt, Abram and Sarai were blessed with money, an increase in their livestock and herds, and they acquired servants and slaves, one of whom was HAGAR. Eventually, Abram and Sarai returned to live in the Promised Land, along with Lot.

FAILING KEY TRIALS LEADS TO THE BEGINNINGS OF TWO MIDDLE EASTERN RELIGIONS

In this section, we will see that the birth of ISHMAEL will lead to the line of the Muslims. The birth of ISAAC leads to the line of the Jews, and eventually the Christians (in a spiritual sense).

After returning to the Promised Land with Abram and Sarai, Lot was captured by some kings, who also lived in the area of the Promised Land. Abram raised a small army and went to war with them, in order to rescue Lot and his family (Genesis 14). Sometime afterwards, Abram asked God who would be his heir, and God reiterated the promises (Genesis 15). But shortly after that, Sarai became very frustrated at not having a son. According to Abram, God promised to give them a son, but over 10 years had passed and she still had not given birth to a child.

Key Spiritual Battle: Whether Abram and Sarai Should Follow Cultural Custom

Trial Overview (Genesis 16:1-4): Sarai convinced Abram to sleep with her maidservant, Hagar, in order to have a son.
1. It was an accepted cultural custom of the time that when a woman was barren; her husband could sleep with a maidservant to have a son. Part of that custom included the lifelong responsibility of the man to protect and care for the maidservant and any offspring.
2. If Abram and Sarai assumed the cultural custom was godly, then they could rationalize the fulfillment of God's first promise by involving Hagar the maidservant.
3. At the time, Abram and Sarai had been back in the Promised Land for about 10 years (Genesis 16:3). Abram was in his mid-eighties.

Reality Check: Sarai was frustrated after 10+ years of hoping for God's promise of a child to be fulfilled. For 10 years it had not happened. During all that time, Abram had gone off to war to save Lot. Perhaps both Abram and Sarai became very aware that they weren't getting younger and that they were living in perilous times! Having a heightened sense of one's mortality can be a strong motivator towards wanting to have children... and quickly.

Discernment Challenge: How To Use Our Role And Influence. A big part of this trial's discernment challenge involved discerning how God would have Sarai and Abram use their role as owners of the maidservant, Hagar. The world said it was OK to fulfill their desire to have a child through Hagar. However, Abram and Sarai had to discern if this was how God wanted His promise fulfilled!

By putting ourselves in Sarai's shoes, we can see that another part of the discernment challenge involved timing. This involved discerning whether God wanted them to have children *when* they wanted the child.

Putting ourselves in Abram's shoes, we can see it can be hard for a man to have to seek God's will and embrace it, especially when it involves telling one's wife, "No, the time isn't right." Husband and wife relationships can be quite challenging when either spouse (or both) are not able to discern God's will or to be content with God's direction.

Trial Outcome: The Tanakh and Bible indicate that neither Abram nor Sarai sought the Lord's guidance concerning their desire to have a child through Hagar. As a result, their decision-making process was impaired from the start. Abram slept with Hagar and they had a son, Ishmael. In this spiritual battle, Abram and Sarai did not "pass the test." Because they had the role as masters over Hagar, they assumed it was OK to use that role to fulfill God's promise of a child. Often times, discerning God's guidance means we should avoid using influence and "power" that we have, though God has allowed us to have it. As a result of failing in this trial, Ishmael was born and a rift eventually arose between the descendants of Ishmael and Isaac. Today we see this chasm in the Middle East conflict.

<u>Key Spiritual Battle: Abraham[**] to Go Against
Cultural Custom</u>

Trial Overview (Genesis 21:1-21): Fourteen years after Ishmael was born, Sarah conceived and had a child. Sarah was highly upset with Hagar because of Ishmael. Sarah wanted Abraham to kick Hagar and Ishmael out.

[**] Note that in Genesis 17:5 and 17:15, God changed Abram's name to Abraham, and Sarai's name to Sarah.

1. According to the cultural custom of the time, Abraham was responsible for the care and welfare of both Hagar and Ishmael because he slept with Hagar. In Genesis 21:11-13, God basically told Abraham to follow his wife's wish and go against the cultural custom that gave him responsibility for the care of Hagar and Ishmael.
2. Abraham was 100 years old when Isaac was born (Genesis 21:5). Ishmael was about 14 years old.

Reality Check: Abraham loved his son, Ishmael. While Sarah was certainly upset about both Hagar and Ishmael, this didn't mean that Abraham wasn't torn over the drama between them. Abraham was greatly distressed and did not want to lose Ishmael. Abraham could have used the cultural responsibility (to care for Hagar and Ishmael) as a seemingly legitimate excuse to go against what Sarah wanted. Were we in Abraham's situation, wouldn't we be praying that God would change Sarah's heart so perhaps Ishmael would be able to stay?

Discernment Challenge: Discerning How To Deal With Other's Perceptions And When To Make A Personal Sacrifice. The challenge of this trial involved discerning how God sometimes wants us to deal with the perceptions of others and when to sacrifice our own desires.

1. **Perceptions of Non-family Members**. While the Bible doesn't say that Abraham had a bunch of friends living in the area, people probably knew him through trading and from living near him. What would people say if they found out he kicked out Hagar and Ishmael? That was considered a "cultural no-no." People find things out. Sometimes our concerns about what others might think can influence our decisions. Discerning guidance from God is challenging when that guidance potentially exposes us to others' negative views and opinions.

    If God was trying to tell you to do something that could make you look bad in others' eyes, could you discern that? Would you be confident that you discerned God's guidance correctly, or would you have lingering doubts and concerns?

Chapter 1: Promise To Crisis

2. **Perceptions of Family Members**. Abraham probably wanted his wife to be happy, but that doesn't mean that her attitude was right in the sight of God. Abraham could have easily rationalized that it wasn't right to make Sarah happy at the cost of doing wrong by Hagar and Ishmael. Wouldn't we wonder whether going along with someone's wrong desire might serve to encourage the person to avoid changing? Wouldn't it make them harder to live with in the future? Wouldn't it seem that Sarah had some responsibility toward Hagar and Ishmael, given that it was her idea for Abraham to have a son through Hagar? Questions like these are normal when we are seeking God's guidance. Sometimes they are legitimate questions, which may or may not lead us to discern God's guidance. However, Abraham's trial shows us that godly discernment goes beyond mere rationalizing and "thinking things through."

3. **Sacrificing One's Desire**. Abraham wanted to be able to keep Ishmael, but could he really accept God's direction if he was being told to give up Ishmael? Perhaps Abraham wondered, "How could a loving God justify directing me to force my son and Hagar to leave? Isn't it wrong to abandon my son?" Again, discernment is about discovering God's direction, not just the direction or response to a trial based on what might initially make sense to us!

Trial Outcome: Genesis 21:12-14 records that Abraham followed God's direction by telling Hagar and Ishmael to leave. God promised Abraham that Ishmael's descendants would be too numerous to count.
1. Abraham "passed the test" by listening to God, yet he did not get what he wanted: to keep his son, Ishmael.
2. Hagar "passed the test," by ultimately trusting God, but she too did not get what she wanted: to be able to stay with her young son under the protection and care of Abraham; to have her son grow up experiencing the love of his father.
3. Sarah did not "pass the test" because her heart was not godly toward Hagar, yet she did get what she wanted: Hagar and Ishmael were kicked out.

While we (as Christians) might view Hagar and Ishmael as "pagans" and "non-believers," an important lesson to note is that God is working with the "pagan" person too. God's love is not restricted to the "godly" people; He loves everyone. Remember that, in Genesis 16:7-9, Hagar discerned that she should return to Sarah. She could have disregarded the angel of the Lord as not being of her particular belief system, but she didn't. She could have rationalized acting differently. However, her heart was inclined toward God. Similarly, we see that God loved Hagar enough to have an angel visit her, the young Egyptian maidservant (Genesis 21:16-19). In sum, the lesson is:

> "God even seeks to communicate to unbelievers and ungodly people. Each trial they experience gives them the opportunity to discover the path God would have them to take. By seeking His will and transforming their hearts in a trial, God can use that godly choice to lead them in the direction which brings them to Him. This is part of what God tried to teach Cain when He said that Cain must "master sin," a task that cannot be done without submitting to God. By making the choice God would have of the person, even ungodly people have the opportunity to *continue* making choices that follow God's lead. In time, this can lead them to embrace the relationship with Him that God hopes they will want. This is actually part of what makes everyone accountable to God: even unbelievers have made *some* godly choices which, if they learn from them, give them proof by their own actions of the importance of a relationship with God!"[1]

Though Abraham followed God's direction to kick out Ishmael and his mom, Hagar, this likely created an opportunity for Satan to attack Ishmael through his life. It looked as though Abraham did not care about Ishmael, as if Abraham wanted to abandon Ishmael. It is not surprising that Ishmael grew up to be an angry man (Genesis 16:12) as a result of feeling rejected by his father, Abraham. Another lesson here is that even though we might follow God's direction in our trials, this sometimes creates a setting for others to experience trials too.

---

[1] *Feelings 102: Bible Studies for LIVING God's Written Word, Volume 1*, William J. Clark, Jr., Keys To Understanding Life Series, September 2013, pages 44-45.

Chapter 1: Promise To Crisis

Other Information About Ishmael and His Line

1. The Tanakh and Christian Bible say the following about Ishmael and his line:
   a. Ishmael's descendants would be "too numerous to count" (Genesis 16:10). The Lord showed favor upon Hagar as a result of Abraham's decision to have a child through her.
   b. Ishmael would be like a "wild donkey" (Genesis 16:12).
   c. Ishmael's line would fight others and others would fight against them (Genesis 16:12, 21:18, 25:18).
   d. Ishmael became a skilled and renowned archer (Genesis 21:20).
   e. Hagar got a wife for Ishmael from Egypt (Genesis 21:21).
   f. Ishmael had 12 sons (12 princes), from whom came 12 tribes (Genesis 25:13-16). Ishmael lived to be 137 years old (Genesis 25:17).
   g. Ishmael settled in present day Saudi Arabia "…in defiance of all his relatives…," (Genesis 25:18).
2. According to Muslim tradition, Hagar and Ishmael went to what is now present day Saudi Arabia. The Qur'an (XXXVII: 100-107), written by Muhammad in 610 A. D., does not mention the name of the child that God told Abraham to sacrifice, but Muslims usually interpret this as being Ishmael and not Isaac, in contradiction to Genesis 22:2.
3. Also according the Qur'an (II: 127-129), Abraham went to visit Ishmael. The Qur'an says that together they built an altar and worshiped God. That altar was located in what is now present day MECCA (in Saudi Arabia). Eventually, Muhammad would build a temple called, "KA'BA," around the site of that altar. (Remember, words in all CAPS are further explained in Appendix 2, starting on page 101.)
4. The Ishmaelites (descendants of Ishmael) traded often with Egypt, and they had a hand in slave trading (Genesis 37:27-28).

Genesis 22-50 details the lives of Isaac, Ishmael, ESAU, JACOB and Jacob's sons. There are many trials for all of them throughout their lives, but the next key spiritual battle we will look at deals with the effect of Jacob's favoritism on his sons and family. It is because of this that the nation of Israel grows up in slavery in Egypt.

Keep in mind that, like Abraham, God changed Jacob's name to Israel (Genesis 32:28). This actually happened before this next trial. Having said that, Genesis still continues to refer to Jacob as Jacob from time to time after Genesis 32. It is because of this name change that the Jewish people, who come from the line of Jacob, become known as the Israelites or the people of Israel (nation of Israel).

Key Spiritual Battle: Jacob's Favoritism Toward Joseph

Trial Overview (Genesis 37): Jacob's favoritism toward Joseph (Genesis 37:3-4) enabled Joseph to become somewhat arrogant when relating the meaning of his dreams to his family. Jacob's favoritism set Joseph's brothers against Jospeh. Joseph was eventually sold to descendants of Ishmael, who were headed to trade in Egypt. Joseph was taken to Egypt and sold into slavery (Genesis 37:28).

Reality Check: Joseph held a special place in Jacob's heart because Joseph was born of his favorite wife and because Jacob was an old man by the time he and Rachel had Joseph.

Another dynamic that encouraged Jacob's tendency toward favoritism was that, from his own point of view, he had had a pretty rough life. While he had taken advantage of his brother, Esau, Jacob had also experienced being taken advantage of by his father-in-law, Laban. Jacob had been cheated and mistreated in much of his adult life, so having been blessed with Joseph at such an old age was very, very special to him. Thus, Joseph became Jacob's favorite son.

Discernment Challenge: Discerning God's Correction. The challenge of this trial was for Jacob to discern God's correction to him when it came to playing favorites. When some people experience tough times, they often overcompensate by clinging all the harder to certain things they have. In Jacob's case, his clinging began by focusing heavily on his wife, Rachel, over his first wife, Leah. Rachel was more beautiful and was Jacob's favorite wife.

Chapter 1: Promise To Crisis

While Jacob's favoritism extended to Joseph, after Joseph was taken away from Jacob, Benjamin was born. Benjamin became the favorite son after Jacob lost Joseph.

Discerning whatever guidance God might have had for Jacob concerning his favoritism had to be challenging because Jacob's favoritism was influenced by his own parents. Jacob's mother, Rebekah, favored him over his brother, Esau. Also, Jacob's father, Isaac, favored Esau over Jacob! Apparently Satan had the upper hand in trials involving favoritism. For Jacob to have been able to discern God's guidance on how to deal with his boys and his wives, Jacob would have had to be willing to let God change the trait of favoritism within himself, which also ran heavily through his family line.

Trial Outcome: By playing favorites, Jacob's failings as a husband and as a father created dysfunction within his own family. Jacob's failure to love each of his boys equally laid a seed that Satan could use to stir up hatred and anger between the sons. Jacob probably didn't discern that his favoritism toward Joseph, at first, and then Benjamin, later on, was not what God wanted. If he did, Jacob didn't let God change him.

Jacob's brother, Esau (and his descendants known as the EDOMITES), remained in the general areas of the Promised Land. Eventually, Jacob and his family went to Egypt (Genesis 46:1-6) because that is where Joseph ended up! In Egypt, Joseph carried great influence and was able to offer food, protection, and safety. Because Joseph ended up in Egypt, the nation of Israel would start growing there. Unfortunately after Joseph died, there would come a time when the new Pharaoh of Egypt saw the people of Israel as a threat and not as friends. This would lead to Jacob's descendants being enslaved for 400+ years... just as God had foretold to Abraham in Genesis 15:13.

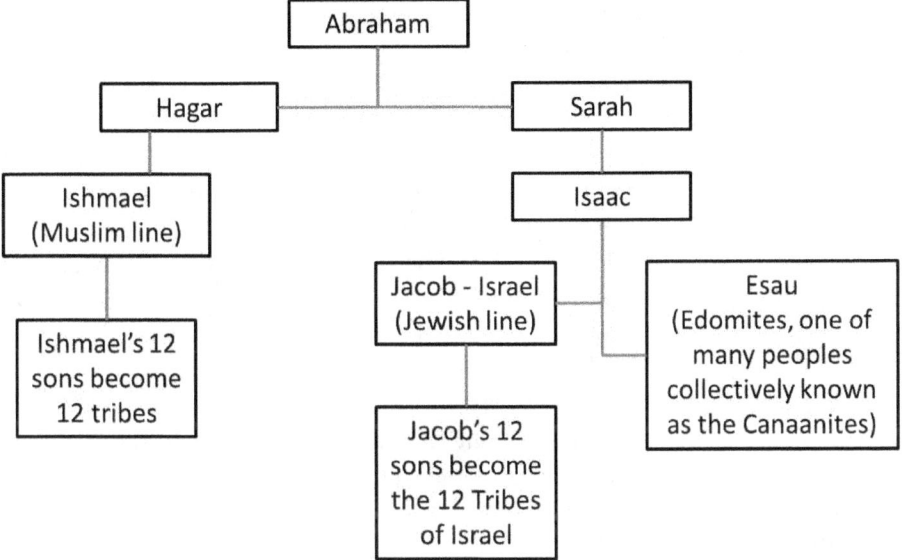

Figure 1.4 – Abraham's Descendants At The Time Of The Exodus

This figure shows the line of Abraham's descendants at the time the Children of Israel made their exodus from Egypt.

<u>Key Spiritual Battle: The Trial of Israel in
Slavery and of Those in the Promised Land</u>

Trial Overview (Exodus 1-12): As the descendants of Jacob grew in number, they were eventually perceived as a threat to the security of Egypt by one of the Pharaohs. As a result, they were enslaved by Egypt. It is likely that the Children of Israel (descendants of Jacob) probably wondered why God allowed them to remain in slavery in Egypt for 400+ years. This trial looks at that.

Reality Check: Why wouldn't God have made the enslavement shorter, perhaps just 10 years, or maybe 20 years? If God loved His people so much, then why would He allow them to be slaves at all?! It certainly doesn't seem fair or loving that God would allow His own people to be enslaved.

Chapter 1: Promise To Crisis

When we ask questions like this about undesirable circumstances in our own lives, we are experiencing a trial. Discerning God's guidance, plan and comfort can be challenging because we normally think, "If God is loving and all powerful, why would He allow such bad things to happen?" This question seems valid, simple and rock solid. And, it is a question that leads many people to conclude either there is no God or that if there is, He certainly isn't loving. Unfortunately, the assumption behind this question isn't valid. The assumption is that this world is supposed to be about fairness, enjoyment, and the *result* of the completion of God's plan.

Remember, Satan was permitted to be in the Garden of Eden (Genesis 3:1-4, 14-15). This indicates that God created mankind in the midst of the spiritual war. One of the ways Satan seeks to fight the spiritual war is by causing us to fail to remember that all things in this world are happening in the context of the greater spiritual war. All aspects of God's plan are not yet fulfilled. Satan began a spiritual war through his rebellion (Isaiah 12:12-14; Ephesians 6:11-13; 1 John 5:19; Acts 26:14-18). Humanity is involved in that war. So, while it is good to enjoy life, we cannot forget that this world is not heaven. Satan was permitted access to God's creation from the very beginning, even *before* the fall. We are not in this world solely for the purpose of enjoyment and fulfillment of our own desires. This world's purpose is to bring glory to God by us choosing to yield our freewill to Him and letting Him live through us in the spiritual battles we face.

In this world, we will face trials and difficulties. The goal isn't to run from that, but to face it realizing there is one thing more important than life itself – service to the Lord out of love for Him and for the sacrifices He's made on our behalf. This is to be a huge part of the Christian's spiritual reality check related to every trial we read about, or that we personally face.

Discernment Challenge: God's Will Includes Others Too; God Sees Fit To Grow And Mold Us. A challenge to discerning why God allowed the Israelites to be enslaved involves seeing the bigger picture from God's point of view. God's will included others, not just the Israelites personally. Similarly, trials and troubles that affect us personally aren't always just about us!

Genesis 15:13-16 says that God was not finished dealing with the people living in the Promised Land. This is very important because it reveals that God's love was not limited to just Abraham and his descendants. God loves all people on the earth. While Jacob's descendants were growing into a nation, God was working with the "pagan people" living in the Promised Land. While God knew the people living in the Promised Land would ultimately reject Him by their own freewill, He still continued to try to reach them through their own trials and difficulties. God could not claim to be fair were the pagan or non-believer not given the opportunity to discern or hear His guidance in their trials too. The issue, however, was whether they would incline their hearts to God in order to do so.

Another discernment challenge for the Israelites concerning their enslavement was that the people of Israel had to realize their need for God and His intervention as they grew as a nation. God was molding and shaping Israel. Unfortunately, we all usually tend to seek God more when we experience difficulty. While the Israelites were certainly mistreated, the Egyptian interest in them as slaves also ensured the Israelites were protected from being completely destroyed by other potential enemies! As slaves, the Israelites also grew together in the course of growing ever larger as a family and nation. The very thing they hated (slavery) held the Israelites together during the nation's infancy. So while there was a negative aspect to slavery in the growth of the nation, being enslaved meant that Israel had to embrace that their freedom and future would be impacted by how well they discerned, as a nation, the leadership and direction of God.

Other challenging aspects of discerning how God was trying to grow and mold the Israelites through slavery can be seen in two parts. First, Jacob's favoritism led to several trials for his family. Again, as a result, Joseph ended up in Egypt, along with Jacob and the rest of the family. This shows us that following God's will for us personally does not imply we are separate from everyone else in terms of trials. In the context of the spiritual war into which we all are born, we are individuals who are also impacted by others.

Chapter 1: Promise To Crisis

Second, the Pharaoh, who was close to Joseph, died and a new Pharaoh came to power. This too was used by God to grow and mold the Israelites, although most certainly Satan also sought to use it to his own ends. The new Pharaoh was not as moved by the past accomplishments of Joseph. The line of Pharaohs who came after was not as close to the descendants of Jacob living in Egypt. This too would eventually lead to Israel's enslavement.

Trial Outcome: There were two big outcomes to this trial for the Israelites and others. First, the peoples living in the Promised Land had centuries of opportunity to discern and follow God; however, as far as we know they did not. Secondly, slavery cauterized the Israelites into a nation of their own… a nation with a common heritage, with the hope of promises from God, and with their own language.

After 400 years of slavery, Jacob's descendants grew to approximately 3,000,000 people. About this time, a man named Moses came on the scene. This was around 550 years after God made the promises to Abraham.

ISRAEL'S EXODUS FROM EGYPT (C. 1450 B. C.)

In this section we will look at how Israel came to be released from Egypt, thus fulfilling what God said in Genesis 15:13-14. This involves key trials for the Pharaoh of Egypt. These trials are an example of some of the challenges that people face in discerning God's guidance when they aren't actually following God.

As the time for Israel's release from slavery drew near, God prepared Moses. Moses faced his own trials, and he would also be a key person in the series of trials faced by the Pharaoh of Egypt at the time.

Key Spiritual Battle: Pharaoh's Economic and National Security Trial

Trial Overview (Genesis 3-15): Pharaoh had several opportunities to discern God's guidance and will concerning the enslaved Children of Israel (Exodus 5:1). The entire story of Moses' interactions with Pharaoh (and Pharaoh's trials) can be found in Exodus 3-15.

Reality Check: By the time Moses comes along with his message from God, the Hebrew people have been Egyptian slaves, under the Pharaoh, for 400 years. That's more years than America is old! When things are a certain way for that many years, change is usually not embraced quickly. The idea of losing the Hebrew slaves presents Egypt and Pharaoh with a very challenging trial! Furthermore, keep in mind that the Hebrews were enslaved in part *because* their population grew so large. Again there were about 3 million in the Hebrew population.

For Pharaoh and Egypt, releasing 3,000,000 people from slavery all at once would have been a gigantic national security and economic risk! As a comparison, just prior to the American Civil War, the approximate number of slaves in the Confederate States was 3.1 million.[2] However, while the slaves in the confederacy were freed by Lincoln, they didn't all leave. In fact, many actually stayed as free citizens after the Civil War was over. Imagine the impact to the economy of the southern states if all the slaves had actually left the south at the same time! This kind of impact was what God, speaking through Moses, was challenging Pharaoh to accept and embrace with an open heart!

But, this wasn't the only discernment challenge Pharaoh faced. While the Lord God tried to get through to Pharaoh, the Egyptian culture was backed by centuries of believing in its own gods, including the idea that Pharaoh himself, and in the Egyptian mind, was a deity in his own right. This was another huge issue in the trial.

---

[2] *Census, Son of the South*, sonofthesouth.net from the 1860 HARPER'S WEEKLY, April 6, 1861. Article "THE CENSUS OF 1860." Retrieved 3/5/2014.

Chapter 1: Promise To Crisis

Moses' lack of worldly qualifications presented another obstacle to Pharaoh's ability to discern God's guidance to him. Moses was relaying to Pharaoh what God wanted. But, Moses was not a king; he was a man from the desert. On top of that, Moses had difficulty speaking well. Moses had to use Aaron to help him communicate with Pharaoh. Pharaoh was dealing with a man, Moses, who, in and of himself, had essentially no meaningful worldly qualifications to support his demands, let alone to claim those demands were from THE God of the Universe! This is a big reality check!

God does use people to communicate truth to others in their trials. When this happens to us personally, sometimes we aren't sure whether to believe the person. Like Pharaoh, we might think, "You are just a person like me, why should I believe God is using you as the instrument to communicate to me? Why can't God just tell me personally what He wants?"

While there have been times God has spoken audibly to individuals and even appeared to individuals, what is always true is that God seeks to communicate to us through our hearts. Part of what made Pharaoh's trials challenging involved being willing to incline his heart to God's message. Pharaoh wanted God's message to align with what Pharaoh wanted and had!

Note that Exodus 4:21, 7:3 and 9:12 say that God hardened Pharaoh's heart. Does that mean that God hardens the heart such that we bear no personal choice or responsibility? The answer is no. We have freewill and play a part in the spiritual hardening of our own hearts. Exodus 8:15, 8:32 and 9:34 each indicate Pharaoh sinned and hardened his own heart! The bottom line is that *Pharaoh* did not yield his heart to the Lord. God let Pharaoh's heart become hardened. The point here is that when we Christians are in trials, if we truly are not willing to discern and cooperate with Gods' will, God designed our hearts such that they will become hardened, at least in that trial.[3]

---

[3] For more about the part we play in hardening or opening our hearts, download or read the free July 2012 edition of "Hearts Up," a discipleship e-publication from KeysToUnderstandingLife.org.

Discernment Challenge: Do What Is Right; God Is In Control.
God loved Pharaoh and the Egyptians as much as He did anyone else. God wanted Pharaoh to follow His lead, particularly concerning the Israelites. To recognize or discern this, Pharaoh would have had to be willing to discern God telling him to do something he did not want to do! God often tries to communicate correction to those He loves!

God's will for Pharaoh was that he release the Israelites. This was the right thing for Pharaoh to do, even though it would likely put great burden and difficulty on Egypt, Egyptian lifestyles and the Egyptian economy. To Pharaoh, the cost of doing what was right seemed too high. He was not willing to imagine that THE God would want such from him. As a result, Pharaoh was unable to discern the wisdom behind releasing the slaves. He was unable to discern that a loving God often asks us to sacrifice what we have or want to Him. This is often an obstacle for us in discerning God's guidance in our own trials!

Pharaoh was also unable to discern that the power he enjoyed over the Israelites was not of his own making, but for serving God's purpose. So, when the Lord's purpose for having Israel enslaved was fulfilled, Pharaoh was unable to discern it was time for change. He was unable to place his faith in God. Each of the plagues, which followed Pharaoh's resistance to God's commands via Moses, were designed to show Pharaoh and the Egyptians that the God of Abraham, Isaac and Jacob was more powerful than anything Pharaoh or his magicians could muster. Pharaoh did not want to admit that there was a God greater than himself, or greater than any other gods in which Pharaoh had believed. Pharaoh's thinking prevented him from discerning God.

Like Pharaoh, whenever we are in a trial, we are being challenged to discern how God wants us to have faith in Him. In some trials that is easier than in others. In all trials, the act of having faith in the Lord will often involve at least an initial uncertainty as to how the Lord will permit the trial to turn out. It always involves acting on a willingness to do what the Lord directs, even when there is great risk or great change involved. In discerning how God wants us to change, we discern a huge piece of the picture of how God is trying to mold and shape us.

Chapter 1: Promise To Crisis

Trial Outcome: After nine plagues and the slaying of the first born, which Israel celebrates annually as The Passover, Pharaoh finally allowed the Israelites to go. The plagues included the turning of water to blood, frogs, gnats, flies, pestilence and death of cattle, boils on man and beast, hail, locusts, and three days of darkness. These are recorded in Genesis 7-13.

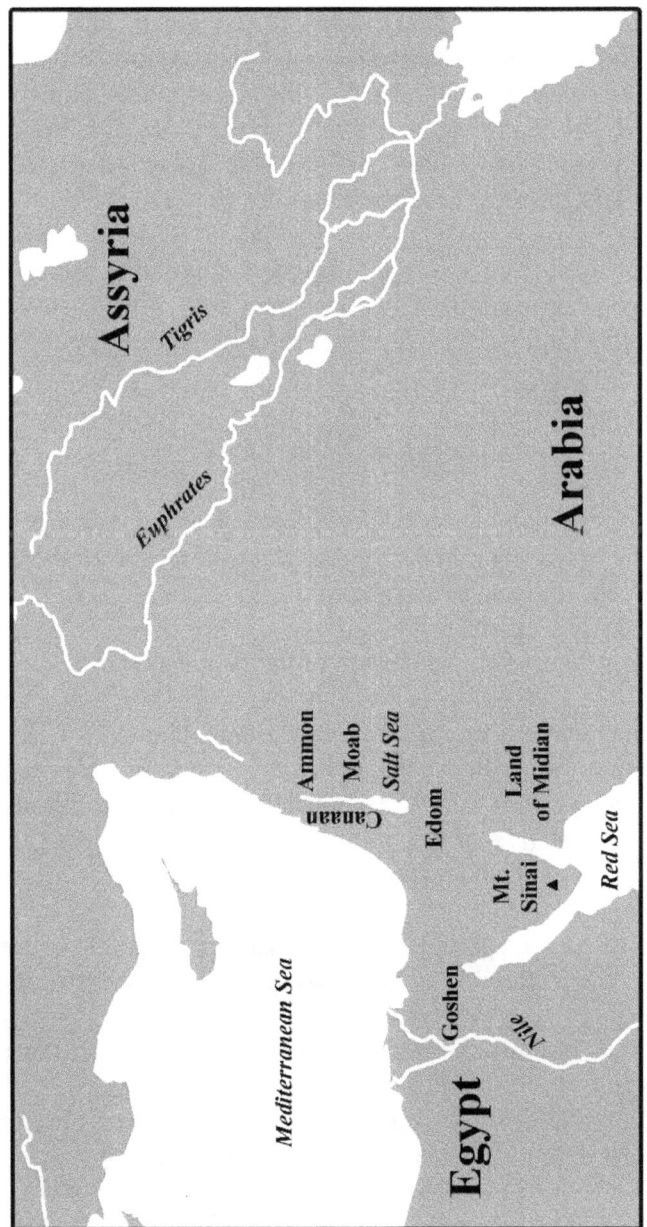

Figure 1.5 – Promised Land At The Time Of The Exodus

This figure shows some of the peoples located in the Promised Land at the time of Israel's exodus from Egypt.

Chapter 1: Promise To Crisis

Prior to each of the plagues, Pharaoh was given the opportunity to discern God's guidance. Pharaoh tried to explain away the natural disasters, but eventually the death of his son convinced him to do what Moses said. While Pharaoh eventually allowed the Israelites to go free, he resisted God again. Pharaoh sent his army after the Israelites (Exodus 14). As a result, his army was destroyed.

Though released from slavery in Egypt, the nation of Israel still faced more trials requiring faith. This happened both when they were in the wilderness and ultimately when they entered the Promised Land itself.

Israel After Slavery

When Pharaoh finally released the slaves, a nation emerged: Israel.
1. They trace their ancestry and claim to God's promises through Jacob, to Isaac, to Abraham.
2. They have their own language.
3. They lay claim to a portion of the Promised Land.

Shortly after leaving Egypt, Moses receives "The LAW" from God at Mount Sinai. Moses eventually writes the Torah, or Pentateuch, which are the first five books of the Hebrew Bible, a.k.a., the Tanakh. These are also the first five of the books of the Christian Bible. Over time, more will be written and added to these Scriptures.

God made three promises to Abraham. Israel claims those promises. The following is how the Jews see those promises being fulfilled:
1. God's promise of a great nation is fulfilled in the nation of Israel.
2. God's promise to bless the world is yet to be fulfilled as, according to the Jews, the Messiah has not come.
3. God's third promise is yet to be fulfilled in that the nation of Israel currently only possesses a portion of the Promised Land. The Israelites, who still believe in God, also believe the Promised Land will one day be possessed in full by Israel.

About 500 years after the exodus (c. 926 B. C.), Israel had a civil war. The nation was split. Israel (the Northern Kingdom) and Judah (the Southern Kingdom) emerged and they never reunited before all of Israel was eventually conquered and dispersed throughout the world in 70 A. D.

JONAH'S TRIAL (782 B. C.)

In this section we will see, once again, God's love for the lost... those who have not yet chosen to follow Him. While the Israelites are referred to as God's chosen people, this does not mean that God didn't or doesn't care for any of the other people on the planet.

<u>Key Spiritual Battle: Jonah Not Wanting To Minister To the Lost</u>

Trial Overview (Jonah 1-4): God cared about the peoples occupying the Promised Land while Israel was enslaved in Egypt (Genesis 15:13-14). Similarly, in Jonah 1 we see that God desired to reach out to "the pagan peoples" of Nineveh, the capitol of Assyria. God chose JONAH to go minister to these pagan peoples. Nineveh was about 500 miles from Jonah's hometown of Gath.

Reality Check: Jonah did not want to take God's message of warning and of love to Nineveh because Jonah was afraid the people of Nineveh would actually respond and get right with God! Jonah didn't want Nineveh to be delivered from God's pending punishments because Assyria was considered one of the Israelites' enemies. If Israel's enemy "got right with God," then God might one day use them to conquer or punish Israel in some way.

Jonah wanted Israel to be the "favorite nation" of God to the extent that they wouldn't experience negative consequences for straying from God. Jonah's story is just one more that reveals God's desire to connect with all peoples. In Jonah 4:4, God asks Jonah what right he had to be angry about the sin of Nineveh. In Jonah 4:11, God replies to Jonah's hatred of Nineveh saying,

> "Should I not have compassion on Nineveh, the great city in which there are more than 120,000 persons who do not know *the difference* between their right and left hand, as well as many animals?"
> (*Italics* are part of translation)

Discernment Challenge: Incline Your Heart To God And Be At Peace With His Will. Jonah clearly overcame the first obstacle in a trial, i.e., being willing to discern God's will. However, Jonah did not want to take the steps of faith he knew God wanted. Jonah initially ran in the opposite direction from Nineveh. When God thwarted Jonah's efforts, he eventually cooperated and delivered God's message to Nineveh. Even still, Jonah failed to incline his heart to God and to be at peace with God's mercy on them.

The people of Nineveh were known to be among the vilest and most violently cruel people. Other empires sometimes referred to Nineveh as the "city of blood" (Nahum 3:1). Nineveh's people and king were challenged to discern God's guidance and open their hearts to Him. This required them to allow God to make major changes in their lives.

One of the key lessons of discernment from Jonah's story is that God does not approve of being angry at others' sin to the point where we actually hate the people and are unwilling to minister to them. We often see the incongruity of other's sinful ways. We often recognize that their hearts are "off" and are filled with self-focus. Nevertheless, we must remember that, like Jonah, we have no real right to be angry. God's written Word reminds us that we have not tended to or created the people we sometimes hate… God has (Jonah 4:10). God alone has the right for such anger. Having righteous anger often feels like it is good and right. However, it is best reserved for the Lord (Matthew 5:43-47).

Externally the challenge for the Ninevites involved believing what one man, Jonah, was saying about their impending doom. Internally and spiritually the Ninevites' trial involved discerning that their lives weren't what God would have them to be.

Trial Outcome: Jonah failed the test. Nineveh passed the test.
1. Jonah understood that God wanted him to go to Nineveh to tell the people to repent. While Jonah discerned what God wanted, his heart was hardened to God's command (Jonah 1:2-3).
2. While Jonah was a servant and prophet of God, which was considered godly (2 Kings 14:25), Jonah had areas in which God challenged him to change and grow personally.
3. Jonah didn't like the people at Nineveh. While Jonah eventually did what God asked, he harbored ungodly judgment in his heart, even after delivering the message God told him to deliver (Jonah 3:7-4:1). On a personal level, Jonah was not victorious in his trial.
4. Nineveh changed its ways, at least for a little while. Nineveh grew in its relationship with God and experienced His love.

Israel After Jonah

1. 722 B. C. Assyria conquered the Northern Kingdom (Israel), and scattered northern Jews throughout the Assyrian Empire. These Jews became known as the 10 lost tribes of Israel because they never returned to the land.
2. 586 B. C. Babylon conquered the Southern Kingdom (Judah). JERUSALEM, including the Temple, was destroyed. While many of the southern Jews were taken to Babylon, a large majority remained in Israel.
3. 536 B. C. Ezra, an Israelite priest, was granted permission to return to Jerusalem with other Jews to rebuild the Temple.
4. By 400 B. C. the Jewish written authority from God was complete in the form of the Tanakh. Basically, this is what is later considered the Old Testament for Christians.

Chapter 1: Promise To Crisis

ISRAEL UNDER THE ROMANS (63 B.C.)

About 60 years before Jesus was born, the Roman General, Pompey, captured Jerusalem. When Pompey took Jerusalem, the priests in the Temple were massacred and the Israelite provinces became subject to Roman rule. This is the point at which the Romans came to be in Israel. The Jews were permitted to continue governing themselves after the Roman takeover. Still, the Jewish-Roman relationship was not always a stable one.

From 20 B. C. – 64 A. D., Herod refurbished the Temple. Israel was still looking forward to the coming of the Messiah. Israel's expectation was that the Messiah would be a kind of worldly king who would reunite Israel, defeat Israel's enemies and restore Israel to a powerful position in the world.

JESUS THE MESSIAH (33 A. D.)

In this section we will see that with Jesus' arrival on the scene, Israel faced trials on both national and individual levels: whether or not to accept Jesus as the Messiah. Jesus as the Messiah represents the fulfillment of God's second promise to Abraham from a Christian perspective – to bless all families (the world) through Abraham's line.

Jesus' message was radical. It was a message of love and sacrifice. He said to love our enemies and to pray for them (Matthew 5:43-48). He cautioned His followers not to judge (Matthew 7:1-6). Contrary to what the Israelites expected, Jesus said He did not come to judge the world, but to save it (John 3:17). Justice for wrongs of this world was not promised until His eventual return (Matthew 12:33-37).

<u>Key Spiritual Battle: Accepting Jesus as the Messiah</u>

Trial Overview (Matthew, Mark, Luke, John): The Israelites were presented with the decision whether to accept Jesus as the promised Messiah both individually and as a nation (John 3:1-21; Acts 10:34-43;

Matthew 23:13-29, 26:59-68, 27:11-26; Luke 22:66-71; John 19:12-15).

Reality Check: Many people had claimed to be the Messiah prior to Jesus. As a result, the Jews were not completely unused to Messianic claims. One of the biggest expectations the Jews had, in terms of being able to recognize the Messiah, was that the Messiah would come as a powerful King in a worldly sense. When Jesus came He taught with supernatural authority and acted with supernatural power; but Jesus still did not meet the expectations of the kind of Messiah/King most Israelites expected. Jesus did not lead Israel with a great army to defeat the Romans. Jesus did not attempt to take the throne in the way the Jews expected (John 18:33-37). These differences were the external parts of the trial facing the Jews.

Often the difficulty we face in discerning God's will and plan deals with how He wants us to respond to a trial. This involves overcoming our external expectations. In trials, we always have to set the external parts of the trial down long enough to look inward and discern God's guidance with our hearts. Satan uses the external parts of a trial to distract and then deceive us. Satan uses the concerns, worries and the issues we have about the external parts of a trial. This is how Satan can get us distracted from the internal spiritual aspects of the trial of which we need to be aware. These internal spiritual aspects of a trial deal directly with our walk with Christ.

Discernment Challenge: Getting Past The External. God's ways and plans don't always look the way we think they might. For example, God directed Abraham to act contrary to cultural customs and what seemed right concerning his son, Ishmael (page 20). God used slavery as a means to grow and shape the Israelites into a nation (page 27). God sent a lowly man with zero external qualifications of his own to represent Him before Pharaoh (page 31). Similarly, the Israelites did not receive a Messianic King that looked anything like what they expected. Accepting that their expectations were off was their biggest challenge to discerning God's will for them.

Chapter 1: Promise To Crisis

God is in charge. In our trials, solid and correct discernment involves opening our hearts to that truth, even with the thought that the fulfillment of our personal expectations may not be part of God's plan!

The Jews' expectations influenced their assessment of Jesus. Unless they opened their hearts to discerning the truth behind the perspectives of which Jesus spoke, they had little chance of getting past Satan's deception via the external parts of their trial. Jesus came with a meek heart and spoke of a relationship with God through Himself. Jesus' focus was not so much on the specifics of the Mosaic Law, but on the spirit of it. He spoke not only of this world, but of the spiritual world behind it. This was difficult for the Jews to deal with, because God Himself gave "The Law," which Israel had embraced for more than 1500 years. Even though the very Scriptures the Jews embraced prophesied about the Messiah, most Jews still could not get past their own expectations and concepts about what the Messiah was going to do for them.

Trial Outcome: Jesus was crucified and rose from the dead. Some Jews acknowledged Jesus as the Messiah (Savior). Some Jews came to believe in Jesus. However, those who did were persecuted not only by the Romans, but also by non-believing Jews. Shortly after Jesus' time on earth, the Lord had Peter relate that the Gospel message was not just for Jews, but for all people. With this, non-Jews were introduced to having a relationship with God through Christ in the heart. While Israel remained God's chosen people, all people were able to be saved through Christ. So essentially, all people had the opportunity to be chosen. The Israelites had not grasped this; in fact to them it seemed to diminish their status with God. Through Christ, God showed He was not favoring one person over another, but favoring all who came to Him. Due in part to persecution, believers in Christ were dispersed throughout the world and began sharing and demonstrating their faith in Christ to others.

<u>Jewish Views of the Messiah</u>

In accordance with Jewish Scriptures, the Jewish views of the Messiah "…embraced 'such doctrines as the … existence of the Messiah; his elevation above Moses, and even above angels; his representative character; his cruel sufferings and derision; his violent death, and that for his people; his work on behalf of the living and of the dead; his redemption and restoration of Israel; the opposition of the Gentiles, their partial judgment and conversion; the prevalence of his law; the universal blessings of the latter days; and his kingdom.' But this same interpretation left out certain elements of greatest and governing importance. The doctrines of original sin and of the sinfulness of man's whole nature were greatly reduced from their Scripture meaning, and practically omitted from the prevalent Jewish teaching. Consequently, the deepest thought of the Messiahship, the salvation of the world from sin, was lacking."[4]

The main Jewish focus was on "kingship and deliverance. And these were chiefly of national significance. The restoration of national glory was the great hope of Israel. All else was subordinate to that. ...the denial has been constant that Jesus is the Christ... the Jews almost universally continued to look for their national deliverer...."[5]

"A feature made prominent at present in Jewish denial of the Messiahship of our Lord is that, in their view, the Old Testament prophecies predict the full and blessed results of the Messianic reign as coming (at the same time) with the Messiah."[6]

By 100 A. D. the Christian written authority from God was completed, but it would not be until 325 A. D. that it took on an early version of today's Bible with the Old and New Testaments assembled together.

God made three promises to Abraham. Christians lay claim to those promises spiritually through Christ. The following is how the Christians see those promises being fulfilled:

---

[4] Unger, Merrill F. *Unger's Bible Dictionary*. 3rd ed. Chicago; Moody Press, 1967, page 718
[5] ibid, page 719
[6] ibid.

Chapter 1: Promise To Crisis

1. God's promise of a great nation is fulfilled in two parts
   a. First, in the nation of Israel.
   b. Second, in that everyone who accepts that Jesus is the Messiah and believes in Him becomes a spiritual descendant of Abraham.
2. God's promise to bless the world is fulfilled in that Jesus is the Messiah.
3. God's third promise is yet to be fulfilled in that the Promised Land will one day be possessed in full by Israel.

ISRAEL DISPERSED (70 A. D.)

Jesus was born, of course, in the midst of the Roman presence in Israel. The New Testament writings reflect the Roman presence throughout Israel. Again, the Jews were able to govern themselves, but there were often conflicts with the Roman presence. What is really interesting is the relationship between the destruction of Jerusalem, the dispersal of the Jews and the overall Jewish rejection of Jesus as The Messiah.

In 70 A. D., Jerusalem is conquered and destroyed by Rome under General TITUS. At this point, Israel had been an established nation for approximately 1520 years. However, Israel had split after its Civil War (in 926 B.C), which divided the Jews into the Northern and Southern Kingdoms. There were only 70 years or so where any of the Israelite nation was in captivity. This occurred under the Babylonians from 605 B.C. – 536 B.C... Still, 1520 years is a long time to exist as a nation.

The Roman victory in 70 A.D. began to disperse the Jews throughout the world. Israel ceased to exist as a geographically-based nation. Peoples from the neighboring regions (Ishmaelites – descendants of Ishmael – and other peoples living in the land of Canaan) went to live in the former land of Israel.

Key Spiritual Battle: Israel Conquered and Dispersed

Trial Overview: The nation of Israel was dispersed by the Romans within one generation of the crucifixion of Jesus.

Reality Check: As a nation, Israel lost possession of its land and was dispersed throughout the world. This opened the door for the descendants of Ishmael to move into and claim the Promised Land.

Rome's dispersion of the Israelites didn't seem connected to their rejection of Jesus years earlier. Perhaps this is because, from the Israelites' perspective, the conquering and dispersion of Israel didn't happen immediately when Jesus was crucified. However, based on the Israelites own history with how God often acts, we see that delays in God's response were not uncommon (Ecclesiastes 8:10–13):
1. Adam and Eve didn't die immediately after eating the fruit from the forbidden tree in the Garden of Eden (Genesis 3).
2. While God was "growing" the nation of Israel in Egypt, He delayed judgment on the Canaanites for four generations (Genesis 15:12-16).
3. God delayed His judgment on Egypt for 400 years while Israel was enslaved there (Genesis 15:11-16)
4. Israel did not obey God by driving the Canaanites out; God often delayed His judgment by a generation (Judges 2:1-5).
5. In 782 B.C., Assyria repented in response to Jonah's message, (Jonah 4:1-3) and God delayed His judgment until 612 B.C. when the next sinful generation of Assyrians departed from His commands.
6. In 597 B.C., Ezekiel prophesied judgment would come against the city of Tyre (Ezekiel 26:1-14). God delayed His judgment on the city of Tyre until 573 B.C. when Nebuchadnezzar conquered the city, and again until 333 B.C. when Alexander the Great actually swept the dust of the destroyed city of Tyre into the Mediterranean Sea.

Discernment Challenge: God Sees Fit To Grow And Mold Us. This trial presented some real difficulties to the nation of Israel in terms of why God would allow them to be conquered and dispersed.

Chapter 1: Promise To Crisis

Israel's discernment challenge lay in connecting the complete conquering and dispersion of Israel to its own rejection of Jesus. Why might that be? Israel had a history of repeatedly being attacked and then being delivered by God. Perhaps Israel's thinking was that God's delivery from Roman dispersion was just around the corner. While the Old Testament itself bears out that whenever Israel was attacked it always involved spiritual issues, Israel had a tendency to fail to appreciate this. Often following generations did not value the lessons learned from previous generations, even though they were often documented in Old Testament Scripture. This problem lent itself to Israel failing to discern that Jesus was the Messiah and then connecting its rejection of Jesus to its dispersion by the Romans. From a Christian perspective, the same is true concerning Israel's ability to recognize Jesus as the fulfillment of so many Old Testament prophecies.

Trial Outcome: As a nation, Israel failed to make any significant shift in its acceptance of Jesus as the Messiah. Israel would not exist as a geographical nation for the next 1878 years.

PALESTINE IS CREATED (66 - C. 135 A. D.)

As we mentioned, around 66 A.D., the Jews began to revolt against Roman rule because they wanted their independence. The war that followed ended about 4 years later, in 70 A.D.; although, it was the just first of three significant Jewish revolts. After the third revolt was crushed (c.135 A.D.), the land of Israel was renamed, "PALESTINE" by the Romans. It remained under this name until 1948.

CHRISTIANITY BEFORE ISLAM (300 A. D. – 634 A. D.)

The New Testament tells much about 1st Century Christianity. In this section we will move forward to look at Christianity after Emperor Constantine and before Muhammad and the birth of Islam. We will also look at a brief overview of the authenticity of the Christian Bible, which came together much as we know it today during this period of time.

Christianity spread throughout the Roman Empire in spite of the persecution of Christians by both the Romans and the Jews. Shortly after 300 A.D., many political repercussions arose due to the conversion of so many people to Christianity. During this time, a Roman Emperor named Constantine became a Christian. There is some controversy as to whether his conversion to Christianity was out of love for Christ and seeking to truly follow Christ, or whether it was a masked political move to quell the troubles in the Empire. Regardless, a couple key events occurred after the conversion of Emperor Constantine to Christ.

In 325 A. D., Emperor Constantine convened the First Counsel of Nicaea and directed it to determine the letters and books to be included in what would become the Christian Bible.

The Authenticity of the Christian Bible

The following is provided as a short and very brief reflection on the uniqueness of the Christian Bible (Old and New Testaments) as God's Word to humanity. This is only an overview.
1. The Christian Bible is an historical document containing spiritual principles.
    - All religious writings contain history and spiritual principles.
    - The history provides the framework which demonstrates the spiritual principles.
    - To evaluate the spiritual principles on their own (i.e., without a historical framework) requires a blind commitment to live one's whole life according to the principles to fully "test" whether or not they work. If there is no historical framework, testing the spiritual principles by living them is the only other basis for seeing if they do what they claim for one's life. For this reason, spiritual principles backed by religious writings with a solid historical framework are more trustworthy.

- If the history, reflected in a religious writing, is generally found to be reliable, then there is a basis for believing that the spiritual principles might be reliable.
- Most religions focus on their spiritual principles, sometimes to the extent of disregarding relevant historical events; as such, their records of history have inaccuracies.
- Judaism and Christianity do not disregard history, but record lots of it. The spiritual truths in the Bible do not conflict with records of history.
- The spiritual principles, associated with the Old Testament and the New Testament, have an objective basis for accepting the spiritual guidance found in this sacred writing. This sets the Christian Bible apart from other sacred writings.
- Genesis thru Esther, Isaiah thru Malachi, and Matthew thru Acts are written as historical records of what happened. That history can be evaluated for accuracy.
- Job thru Song of Solomon and Romans thru Revelation contain historical references that clarify and illustrate the spiritual principles. That history can also be evaluated for accuracy.

2. Tanakh and Christian Biblical history and scientific facts are remarkably accurate. The following (which is not a full list at all) are a few facts which have been documented by other ancient records and/or today's scientific community.
    - Leviticus 17:11 (Life is in the blood)
    - 2 Kings 17:1-8; 18:13-16; 19:32-37 (Jerusalem's deliverance from Assyria)
    - Psalm 8:8 ("Paths in the sea" – ocean currents)
    - Isaiah 13:19-22 (destruction of Babylon)
    - Ezekiel 26:3-5 (destruction of Tyre)
    - Micah 5:2-3 (Bethlehem as birthplace of the Messiah)
    - Malachi 3:1-2 (prophecy of John the Baptist)
    - Matthew 24:1-2 (destruction of the Temple – 70 A.D.)
    - Luke 2:1-3 (Census requires returning to family home)

3. The Tanakh and Christian Bibles have been preserved over time.

- The New Testament was originally written in Greek. No ancient secular writing (i.e. those by Julius Caesar, Plato, Sophocles, Aristotle, etc.) is documented by as many surviving manuscripts as the New Testament.
- From 150-400 A.D. the New Testament was translated into Syrian, Egyptian Coptic, and Latin. If, hypothetically, no ancient manuscripts of the New Testament in Greek existed today, the New Testament could still be recreated from the translations that existed by 400 A.D.!
- The Church Fathers (133-340 A.D.) wrote many books on the Christian faith. In those writings they quoted from the ancient manuscripts. Again, hypothetically, if no ancient manuscripts of the New Testament in Greek existed today, the New Testament could largely be recreated from the quotations found in the writings of the Church Fathers.
- The only ancient writing documented better than the New Testament is the Old Testament.

In February 27, 380 A. D., the Roman Empire took the Trinitarian Version of Christianity as the official State Religion. Constantine the First began building Christian Holy Sites within Jerusalem. Jerusalem was declared a Christian City! Jews were not allowed within the city of Jerusalem; if found within the city, the penalty for a Jew was death. **Around this time period, the expansion of Christianity throughout the Roman Empire effectively led to Christian control of the Promised Land!**

Chapter 1: Promise To Crisis

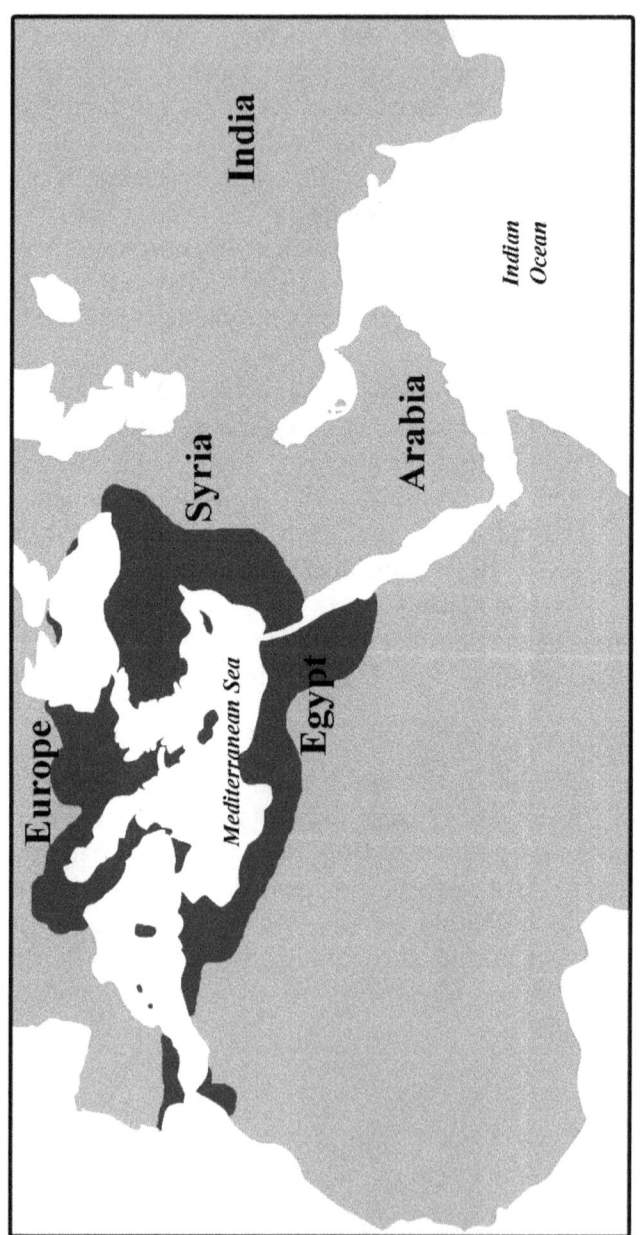

Figure 1.6 – Spread Of Christianity, c. 600 A.D.

The dark shaded part shows a general outline of the spread of Christianity by about 600 A.D., just before Muhammad and the beginning of Islam.

MUHAMMAD AND THE BIRTH OF ISLAM (610 A. D.)

On April 22, 570 A. D., Muhammad was born. Muhammad claimed to be a descendent of Ishmael. He claimed to have received the first of his revelations from God at Mecca, which is located in present day Saudi Arabia. Muhammad and Islam claim the following to be true:
1. God called Muhammad to be the Last Prophet.
2. God made revelations to Muhammad, which were recorded in The Qur'an. The Qur'an is the ultimate truth and surpasses all other previous revelations from God (which would include the Tanakh and Christian Bibles).
3. Mecca was identified as the center of the world. According to Islam, Mecca is where Abraham and Ishmael built an altar (the KA'BA) to worship God. Mecca is the first of three key holy cities in Islam. (Remember, words in all CAPS are further explained in Appendix 2, starting on page 101.)

At the time Muhammad said he received his revelations from God, there was no state or geographic nation of Israel. The Israelites had been dispersed throughout the world (by Rome) for over 500 years. At the time of Muhammad, the Promised Land was occupied by descendants of Ishmael and other peoples. There were some Jews living there and some may have owned property, but they were not in control of any of the Promised Land in any significant way.

According to Muhammad, once he received the revelations he went to some Jews living in Mecca and told them about the revelations. He was thinking the Jews would embrace them. Remember, this is because Muhammad believed that God, i.e., the God of the Jews... the God of Abraham, Isaac and Jacob, was the same God Who gave him the revelations (the Jewish, Christian and Muslim views of God was first discussed on page 4). However, the Jews rejected Muhammad and his revelations, and they ran him out of town.

After having to flee Mecca, Muhammad went to MEDINA (located in present day Saudi Arabia). The people of Medina embraced the revelations, and Muhammad was able to raise an army. Muhammad returned to Mecca, took it by the sword, and cleansed the altar of Abraham and Ishmael. Because Medina was the first to embrace

Chapter 1: Promise To Crisis

Muhammad's revelations, Medina is considered the second of the three key holy cities for Islam.

By 656 A. D. the Qur'an was completed. Peoples of the Arabian Peninsula and beyond were converted to Islam, often but not always by the sword. Various translations of the Qur'an were made in other languages. However, in Islamic worship, the Qur'an is only to be read in Arabic. When peoples are converted to Islam, if they are "dedicated" they will learn enough Arabic to read and speak from the Qur'an in the language in which it was claimed to have been given to Muhammad – Arabic.

Muslim tradition says that in a vision Muhammad was taken to heaven on a white horse. The last place on earth that the white horse's hoof was to have touched was a rock in Jerusalem. For this reason, Jerusalem is the third of the three holy cities in Islam. Today, at the location of the rock, is a mosque. It is called, "The DOME OF THE ROCK."

God made three promises to Abraham. Muhammad saw these as being passed down to him through Ishmael, and so Muslims claim the promises to Abraham. The following is how Muslims see those promises being fulfilled:
1. God's promise of a great nation was fulfilled in that the peoples of the Arabian Peninsula and beyond can be converted to Islam.
2. God's promise to bless the world was fulfilled through Muhammad.
3. God's third promise was fulfilled in that the Promised Land was possessed in full by Islamic peoples (by 661 A.D.).

Muhammad began converting the Arabian Peninsula to Islam during his lifetime, but he died in 632 A. D. However, the Islamic wars for spreading Islam continued after his death (and the recording of his revelations continued until 656 A. D). Meanwhile, in 634 A. D., two years after Muhammad's death, Muhammad's successors lay siege to the city of Jerusalem. Christians (as part of the Roman Empire) possessed the city at the time, but they lost it to Muslim armies.

MUSLIM CIVIL WAR (650 A. D.)

In 650 A.D., the Muslim world was divided over who should be Muhammad's successor and how to interpret the Qur'an. Two key Islamic persons arose in the Civil War. This caused the Muslim world to split.
1. ALI IBN ABI TALIB said the Qur'an is to be interpreted by Muhammad's teaching and practice and that an IMAM did not have to be a direct descendant of Muhammad. The Imam can be elected as a Caliph. Followers of Ali became known as ***SUNNIS***.
2. ABU BA'KR said the Qur'an is to be interpreted only through a direct descendent of Muhammad. Followers of Ba'Kr became known as ***SHIITES***. Most Shiites believe that to be a good Muslim, one has to follow an Imam, a leader of worship, who is in the direct bloodline of Muhammad. Shiites consider Ba'Kr to be the first legitimate Imam and the first true Caliph.

God made three promises to Abraham, which the Muslims claim. The Sunnis and Shiites are the two largest "denominations" within the Muslim faith. Generally speaking, the various Islamic denominations hold to Five Pillars of Faith, which are five key tenants, if you will, of their faith. As such, various Islamic denominations agree on the status of the three promises according to Muhammad, but they disagree on other things, such as how to interpret the Qur'an as seen in the two points above. Again, the areas in which Muslims disagree have led to sharp divisions, often of hatred and hostility, even within the Muslim world.

Today, an estimated 75-90% of the Muslim world is Sunni; the next largest "denomination" is Shiite making up approximately 10-20% of Muslims. The percentages of each vary within countries of the world (see Appendix 1, page 99). Throughout the world there are many who have been converted to Islam. Also, many Muslims have immigrated throughout the world, especially to England, France and the United States.

Of the two main Islamic "denominations," the Shiite tends to be stricter and more fundamental in their application of Qur'an teachings to daily living than is the Sunni. This is because Shiites see their Imam

Chapter 1: Promise To Crisis

as having to be in the direct bloodline to Muhammad, Ishmael, and Abraham. Shiites also tend to be less tolerant toward non-Muslims. Having said that, extremists in any of the Muslim denominations are more fanatical and stricter in the application of their Islamic views than is the mainstream Islamic believer. This is often true even when the mainstream believer is of the same denomination as the extremist.

By 661 A. D. Muslims occupied the Promised Land in full. They would continue to do so for approximately the next 1338 years. Muslim possession of the Promised Land would continue until Israel came back as a nation in 1948. The Muslim possession, and later its loss, of the Promised Land is one of the main sources of conflict within the Middle East today.

DRUZE AND THE SHIITE CONTROVERSY (1017 A. D.)

In 912 A. D, there was a conflict among the Shiites and the lead Imam (Shiite) of the time was killed. His son would have been the next Imam in the line. However, his son was taken into hiding and was not seen again. This began what is known as the "Hidden Imam." This is the person whose return the Shiites are still waiting for today.

In 1017 A. D., an Imam "appeared" and claimed to be the Hidden Imam. He also claimed to be a deity. Most Shiites rejected this Imam and persecuted those who believed in the deity of that Imam. However, a small group of Shiites accepted this Imam, and they become known as the DRUZE.

Shiites and the Druze are both "denominations" within the Muslim faith. As such, they agree on the status of the three promises according to Muhammad; they disagree on the proper lineage of Imams that succeeded Muhammad. This difference led to a small but sharp split within the Shiite denomination of Islam.

Druze is a very small group of Shiite Muslims. They tend to be very quiet and secretive about their faith. On the whole, they are not very militant. Still, most often a Druze won't even talk to someone about their faith, as they interpret the Qur'an to mean that non-believers are forever and hopelessly ignorant.

There are many other small denominations that have come out of the Sunnis and Shiites. Almost all of them are persecuted to some extent or another, but often this depends heavily on what is going on at the time in a given country.

Chapter 1: Promise To Crisis

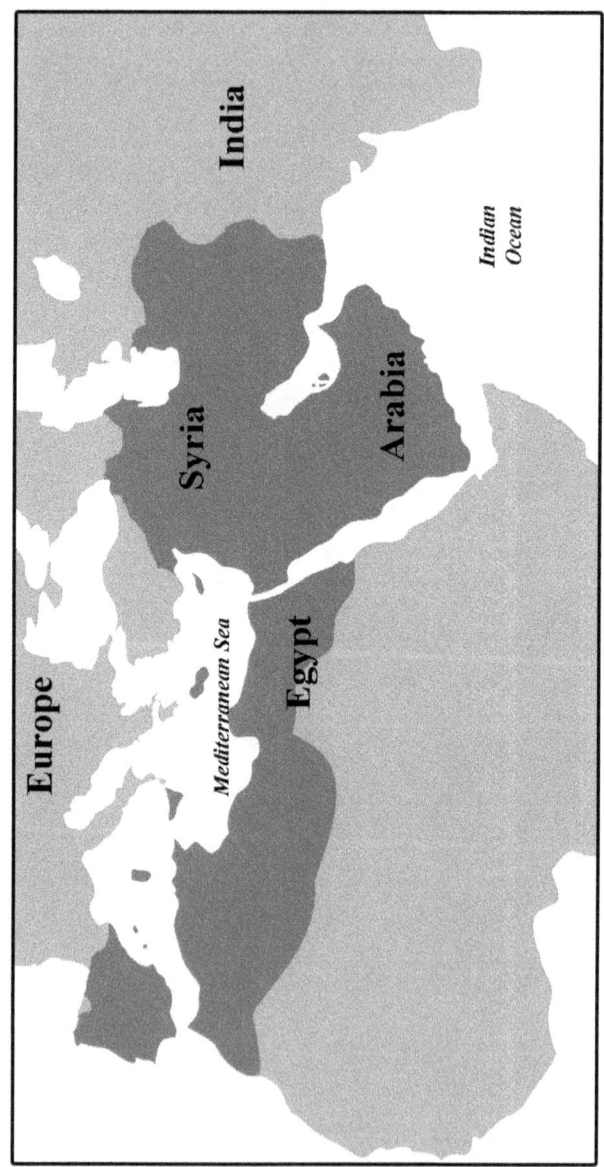

Figure 1.7 – Spread Of Islam c. 900 A.D.

The dark shaded area in this figure shows the spread of Islam over the 300 years after Muhammad. Note that it includes full control of the Promised Land. You may want to compare this figure with Figure 1.6 (page 50), which shows the spread of Christianity c. 600 A.D. You'll notice that Islam became influential in most of the areas that were once Christian.

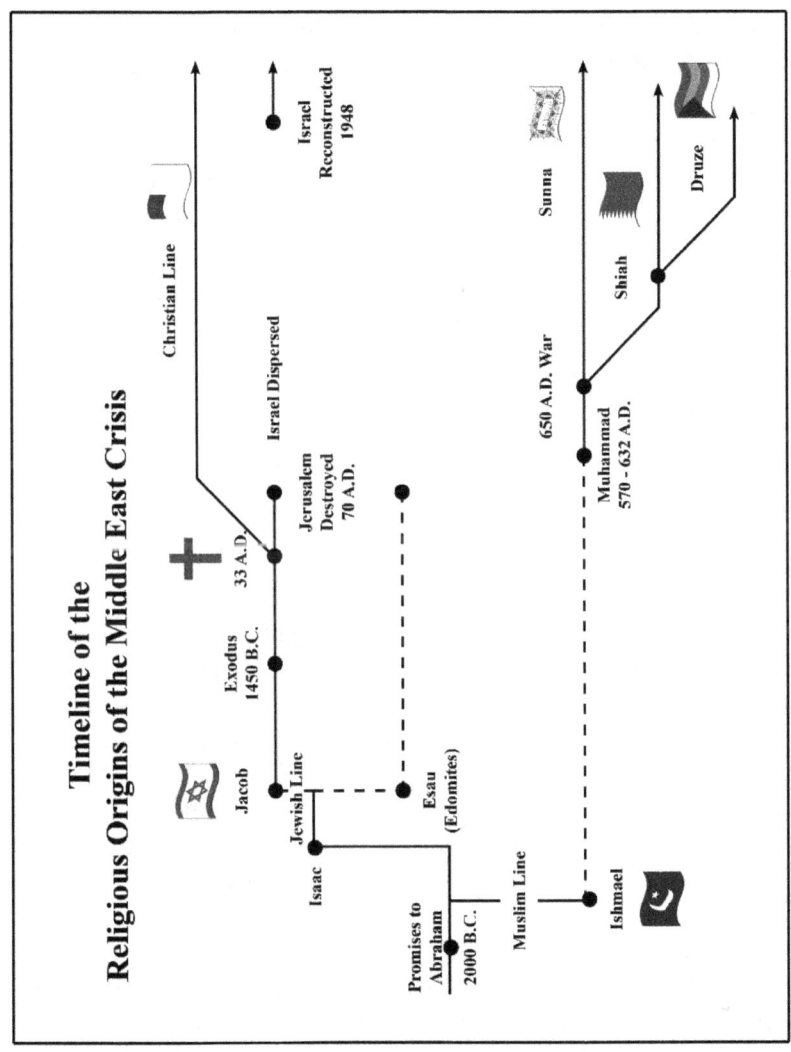

Figure 1.8 - Timeline of the Religious Origins of the Middle East

CHRISTIANITY AFTER 1054 A. D.

Up to about 1054 A.D. there were no significant splits in Christianity, although the size of the Christian world was large. However, in 1054 A. D., Christianity split over political differences between countries in

Chapter 1: Promise To Crisis

Europe and the Middle East. This led to distinctions which came to be known as Western versus Eastern Christianity. The Western Church was the Roman Catholic Church. The Eastern Church became known as the Eastern Orthodox Church. In Europe, the United States and other western nations, most Christians can trace their roots through the Western Church.

Key Spiritual Battle: Convert, Leave, or Die

Trial Overview: Around the 9th and 10th centuries, the Roman Empire was in decline. The split of the Christian Church didn't strengthen the Western Church (Roman Catholic Church). With the decline, the Church in the west began to lose its influence and power. What's more, a significant minority of the European continent was Jewish or Muslim.

Reality Check: Christians in Europe began to see the Jewish and Muslim portions of the population as a significant influence at the same time the Church's influence was weakened by the split of the Church. The Christian Church (Western Church) was clearly the religious power of the day in Europe. Still, there arose an opportunity to use the fact that Jews and Muslims were non-believers as a means to strengthen the center of power in the Christian Church. The Christian leadership wanted Jews and Muslims out of their countries.

Discernment Challenge: How To Use Our Role And Influence. The trial the Church leadership faced involved the temptation to use its power and influence in a way that built on the tendency to act on one's hate of one's enemies... in this case, the Jews and Muslims. This is clearly not among the teachings of Christ (Matthew 5:43-47). Still, the weakening of the Church was real and unnerving for Church leadership. To discern how to avoid misusing their God-given power and influence, believers had to be willing to leave the future of the European Church in God's hands. This meant they had to be at peace with God concerning a possible worst case scenario: that God's will might be to allow the European-centered Western Church to be replaced by someone or something else greater in power!

Trial Outcome: On the whole, the Western Church failed to pass this trial. In August 1096 A. D., Christians in the west mounted the First Crusade, which pitted Christians against Jews and Muslims in European countries. Similar trials continued off and on in different ways for about 400 years. Many events happened as a result of Christians' actions independent of God.

Over 10,000 Jews were killed in the first month of the First Crusade. By the time it ended, an estimated 1.2 million Jews were killed by Christians during this crusade. Over the next 400 years, Jews were killed or kicked out of France, Germany, England and Spain.

Other crusades followed the First Crusade. This time in history is often referred to as "The Medieval Ages" or "The Dark Ages." The Church's crusades were later directed against the Muslim occupants of the Promised Land, in an attempt to re-establish Christian control over the Promised Land and the Holy sites in Jerusalem. In the end, the Muslims retained control over the Promised Land, although they were continually persecuted, displaced or killed in Christian Europe. The Muslims haven't forgotten this part of the Christian-Muslim relationship. While it happened a long time ago, it carries influence in today's Middle Eastern Crisis.

Another result of the Western Church's failure to resist the temptation to misuse its role, power and influence was that it opened the door for the Western Christian Church itself to fracture. Off and on through the Dark Ages many, many wars were fought on the European continent. Because some of the battles ended up being among Christians themselves, a number of denominations formed within the Western Christian world. In almost all of the wars fought between Christians in Europe, Christians on both sides prayed to the same God for deliverance from the other side, and for their side's victory! The Western Christian Church was decidedly fractured as a result of the Christian Church's trial in the 9th and 10th centuries.

Another significant event that happened during the Church's persecution of Jews and Muslims was what we today call, "The Little Ice Age." The weather in Europe became extremely cold, killing off

Chapter 1: Promise To Crisis

crops and inducing widespread famine and disease. Christians, Jews and Muslims alike died by the millions due to this "natural" disaster.

While the Church accepted Jesus as the Messiah, the Church conducted itself independently of God in big ways during its trials. And, the Church's influence in the governing of Europe more or less came to an end with what we now call, "The Renaissance." This period of history saw the further weakening of the Church as a result of interest in secular pursuits such as intellectualism, humanism, and exploration and expansion of secular government power. While some Christians took advantage of the results of exploration to expand mission work and to seek refuge from persecution by the Roman Catholic Church (Western Church), most pursuits defining the Renaissance period arose in response to the Church's poor handling of its own trials. Many people were turned off by the Church, and God became heavily replaced by human creativity and reasoning.

While the Renaissance brought the Dark Ages to a close, the results of the Church's actions placed Christianity well against both Jew and Muslim until World War I.

Christians Relate to Jews in Light of Old Testament Israel

The relationship between primarily Christian countries and the Jewish people began to soften during World War I. Christian western nations eventually sided heavily with the Jewish people at the end of World War II, as well as with the Israeli desire to re-form their nation in the Middle East.

An issue during and after WWII, both by the Allies and the Axis powers, was the military need to secure oil deposits in the Middle East. In sympathy of the wrongs done to the Jews in WWII, and in part with the rise of the key role that oil played in today's world, the West, as well as the U. N., supported the formation of a part Jew and part Arab state. That state was to be created in what was then the British-controlled land (colony) of Palestine.

ISRAEL IS RESTORED (1948)

World War II ended in 1945. The Jewish holocaust was exposed, and an estimated six million Jews were found to have been exterminated. During and after the war, many Jews began moving to Palestine for refuge. (Remember, Israel was renamed Palestine by the Romans, page 46.) The Palestinians were (are) mostly Muslim. The dramatic migration of Jews to, what they considered the Promised Land, renewed the historical tension in the region. While the Muslims were strongly against what they considered to be a Jewish occupation, the world was confronted by the persecution of the Jews during World War II. In general, the non-Muslim world (in some instances, reluctantly) supported the formation of the State of Israel in 1948.

In light of the holocaust during World War II, the gathering of Jews in Palestine was so great that on October 29, 1947 the United Nations recognized Israel's right to exist as a nation with land. Today, the land (country) previously known as Palestine is now known as Israel.

On May 14, 1948, Israel declared itself to be a sovereign nation. This ended Israel's 1878 years of being dispersed after Rome conquered Israel in 70 A. D. **For the first time in human history after being dispersed for so long**, a people came together with...
    a.   ...their language.
    b.   ...their religious history.
    c.   ...their culture.

ISRAEL TODAY (1948 - PRESENT)

While the State of Israel exists today, it is not the same as the Israel we read about in the Old Testament. The judicial branch of the current Israeli government is made up "...of English common law, British Mandate regulations, and Jewish, Christian, and Muslim religious laws."[7] Today's State of Israel is not built upon "The Law" given by God and passed to Moses, as it once was prior to being conquered by

---

[7] *Israel: The World Factbook.* Central Intelligence Agency. 26 February 2014. Retrieved 3 March 2014

Chapter 1: Promise To Crisis

Rome in 70 A.D. Today, Israel is a secularized, democratic nation, separated in function from its religious roots. Israel functions similarly to America in that it attempts to be guided by moralistic principles they perceive as applying to humanity, as opposed to being guided by principles God put forth either in the Tanakh or New Testament.

Today's Jews are not all advocates or followers of Judaism. For many Jewish people, they trace their lineage to Abraham and they call the lands in and around Israel home, but they do not necessarily practice Judaism or hold to the teachings of the "Jewish Bible," The Tanakh.

As a result of the official formation of the nation of Israel, war erupted from the tensions in Palestine. Many Muslims were displaced into refugee camps. Many Palestinians were expelled from Israel. As a result, the Palestinian Liberation Organization (PLO) was formed with the goal of removing Israel from Palestine.

Muslims view the restoration of Israel into part of the Promised Land from the perspective that God had already fulfilled all three promises through Muhammad and Islam (page 52). From the Muslim extremist point of view, Israel, along with its supporters like the United States and some European nations, has undone the very promises of God. To the Muslim extremist, it is wrong, or sinful, to allow Israel and her supporters to maintain a foothold on the Promised Land because, in the Islamic view, this violates the very promises God made to Abraham.

Another result of the official formation of the nation of Israel is a series of brief, quite violent, and intense wars between Israel and its Muslim neighbors. You can Google the following to learn more.
- The War of Independence 1948-1949
- Campaign of the Sinai 1956
- The Six Day War 1967
- The Yom Kippur War 1973
- The Lebanon War 1982

As a result of the ever-changing conflicts and political climates in the Middle East, there have been a number of Islamic movements, some of which have led to the formation of other terrorist groups. It is not uncommon that many of the movements, which ultimately become

Religious Origins of the Middle East Crisis, 2nd Edition

associated with terrorism, began as movements for humanitarian aid, hospital and school building, etc. for different Muslim and Palestinian communities and/or sects (denominations).

Appendix 2 (Definitions starting on page 101) includes a few definitions of some of the movements often associated with terrorism and Islamic extremism:
- AL-QAEDA
- HAMAS
- HEZBOLLAH
- MUSLIM BROTHERHOOD
- ISIS (Islamic State of Iraq and Syria), a.k.a. ISIL (Islamic State of Iraq and Levant)

Chapter 1: Promise To Crisis

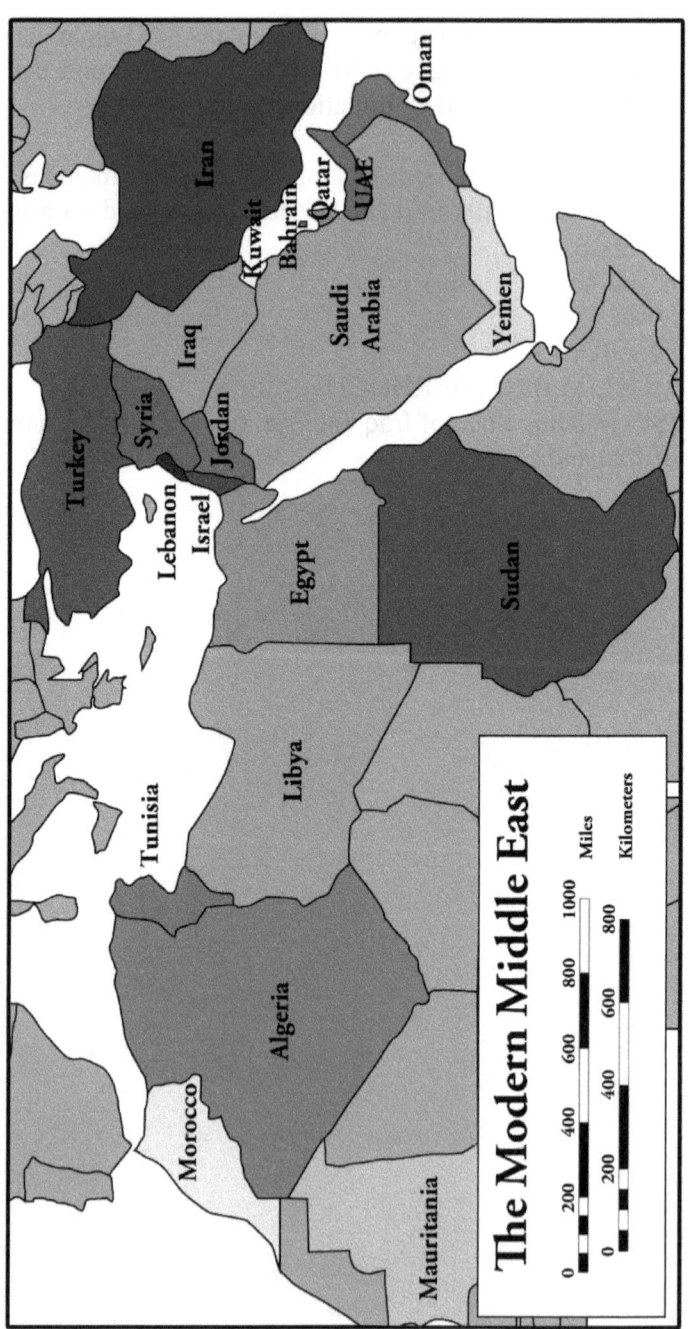

Figure 1.9 - The Middle East At About 2014 A. D.

Chapter 2: The Present Situation

Scope

The present situation in the Middle East seems to be changing in one way or another practically every day. New groups continually emerge in the Middle East. New attacks, alliances and issues constantly add to and fuel the crisis. Yet in spite of all the continual flux and change we see in the Middle East, there are some consistencies we can observe. At the core of all the external conflicts and dynamics we witness in the Middle East are some consistencies in the nature of the relationships between Jews, Christians and Muslims.

When we look at today's relationships between the Jews, Christians, and Muslims, there are many issues and dynamics that influence those relationships. It is very important to realize that, for those of us who live in Western nations (particularly in America), the statements by our political leaders and media news are often the sources from which we develop our understanding of those relationships. These sources typically convey and describe issues concerning peoples of other religions mostly from the perspective of *political* differences. This can actually create more misunderstandings for the Christian population at large, in terms of getting our focus on the external, as opposed to the internal spiritual dimensions of the conflict. It also promotes the inefficiency of America's "religiously-neutral" approach to diplomacy and problem-solving in dealing with the Middle East crisis. America's problem-solving is based on politics and does not follow the direction of God according to any one faith.

Differences In Problem-Solving

It is important to note that what follows in this section does not just apply to American politicians or Western politicians. It applies to all politicians who are not Muslim. It can include American politicians,

Chapter 2: The Present Situation

European politicians, African politicians, Russian politicians, Israeli politicians, etc. Keep this in mind as you read.

For the Muslims, underneath all the external issues and conflicts are a number of religiously-related and historical issues that matter to the Muslim point of view. Non-Muslim politicians often don't see, understand or desire to deal with these religiously-related and historical issues because many countries work to separate Church from State, as does America.

Overview of Challenges for Non-Muslim Politicians

Needless to say, there are many challenges for non-Muslim politicians when it comes to both foreign and domestic policy making. Much can be said here, but we'll focus on four specific challenges:
1. Problems for Christian politicians.
2. The illusion of Muslim political leaders.
3. Problems in believing a Muslim leader's word.
4. The challenge of recognizing a Muslim leader's intentions.

Problems for Christian Politicians

Some of the things we talk about here aren't easy. We need to touch on a couple things, not to slander Christian politicians, but rather simply to make a few things clear about the position they are in as politicians.

While a politician might personally be a Christian, by virtue of his political position he will tend to approach problem-solving first as a politician/diplomat.* Christian politicians *generally* do not always

---

* Again, remember that, generally, politicians in Western nations, including America, function first from a political perspective – not from personal religious views. For Western nations, when a nation's military is directed to take action, this happens as part of that nation's political problem-solving processes. In most modern nations, military action is fundamentally an extension of a nation's political will. While this also applies to Muslim nations, we must remember that the religious leaders in Muslim nations (both Sunni and Shiite) usually direct (and

approach our country's problem-solving based on their own personal religious views. From a worldly perspective, this is appropriate because they are to represent the greater population who elected them, many of whom are probably NOT Christian. Naturally then, politicians generally do not use their political platform to specifically exercise and/or persuade others to act on their personal particular religious views.

The Illusion of Muslim Political Leaders

For Muslims, it is exactly the opposite. Religious views and history influence how Muslims function politically. For Muslims, religious leaders determine what political leaders must say and do in order to exercise and further the Muslim faith. Sometimes the top political leader of a Muslim nation or organization is the top religious leader too. However, in many cases, in a Muslim nation or organization, the top leader who is "in charge" is primarily "in charge" in a political sense. This is the person whose name is usually known to the world. But, in many cases, behind that leader is an Imam, a religious leader, or a counsel of religious leaders, who must tell or bless what that leader says or does. What comes out of the leader's mouth has frequently been decided by the Islamic religious leaders of that country or organization. So often the political leader at a negotiating table is not THE leader at all but rather a messenger... it is an illusion. This is somewhat similar to the early relationship between Western European kings and the Church at the beginning of the Medieval Ages; although

sometimes dictate) the political decisions made by Muslim politicians. A Muslim nation's political decisions are mostly religiously based!

We have to remember that Muslims don't problem-solve according to non-Muslim values! Because of the integral part that religious beliefs and views play in Muslim problem-solving, individual Muslims (both Sunni and Shiite) often take "military-like actions" independent of their nation's official directives. In most Western nations, we call these actions "terrorism." But, because religious views determine a Muslim's political views, "terrorists" often claim to be combatants in war. The war they speak of is not one which is necessarily declared by a particular country (which would be political to a westerner), but which they view as being demanded by their religious beliefs. For Muslims, going to war isn't as much about politics or economics as it is about religious beliefs. For non-Muslim nations, it is the other way around.

Chapter 2: The Present Situation

this relationship broke down eventually in Western Europe in the Renaissance Period. It has NOT significantly broken down in Islam since c. 600 A.D.

Problems in Believing a Muslim Leader's Word

One of the frustrations that non-Muslim diplomacy often encounters with Muslim leaders is that Muslim leaders sometimes say one thing, and then later they do another. Most modern nations view this as lying... as an act that breaks down trust and diplomacy. But for Muslims, saying one thing to a non-Muslim and doing something else can be very appropriate and even "godly" as far as it can be consistent with Islamic teachings. Why is this?

The Qur'an makes strong distinctions between those who believe in God (in light of Islam) versus everyone else. In and of itself, this is not different from the Tanakh or the Bible. However, many passages in the Qur'an are interpreted or emphasized by some Muslim religious leaders as justification for national or extremist leadership to lie to non-believers (Muslim enemies). One of the values and purposes for a Muslim to lie is in gaining the trust of their enemy. The purpose is to cause their non-believing enemy to put themselves in a vulnerable position in which they can be attacked, defeated, converted or killed. The prerequisite for a Muslim's lie to be justified and "righteous" is that it must further the cause of Islam. Muslim national leaders or extremists may often enter into an agreement or treaty with non-Muslims and be considered righteous when that agreement or treaty is used only to weaken the Muslim's enemy or non-believing opponent. Some such passages that are interpreted to support these kinds of actions are Qur'an 3:54, Qur'an 16:106 as well as several references in the HADITH.

The Challenge of Recognizing A Muslim Leader's Intentions

It is important to note that such interpretations of the Qur'an might or might not be embraced by the everyday Muslim on the street. They are, however, frequently embraced by Muslim national or political leaders and in extremist organizations.

Some Muslims view JIHAD, or Holy War, as mainly an internal struggle to let God live through them. This view has similarities to the Christian view where spiritual battles are a "...struggle not against flesh and blood, but against the rulers, against the authorities, against the powers of this dark world and against the spiritual forces of evil in the heavenly realms" (Ephesians 6:12).

Other Muslims view jihad as the external struggle against anyone, or any system that is not according to their Islamic beliefs or particular Muslim denominational beliefs. A challenge for non-Muslim politicians is in figuring out which Muslim leaders hold which views. This isn't as easy as it might seem.

Muslim leaders can be selfish just like any Christian or Jew. Nobody is completely selfless but Christ. Christians and Jews have been known to lie too. Some Muslim leaders have been known to lie to keep their positions of power more so than for the furthering of Islam. Christian and Jewish leaders have lied to keep their positions of power for selfish reasons too. But, there is a difference when many Muslim leaders or extremists lie. Again, the difference deals with their religious beliefs. The difference is that Muslim political leaders or extremists (who lead based on the direction of Muslim religious leaders) are permitted to lie as long as the purpose is to further Islam. In this case, "furthering Islam" means establishing Islam, by force or manipulation, if necessary, over all other belief systems and over all other faith groups. In these situations, no matter how it appears at first, the Muslim leadership is ultimately seeking or posturing for a global and universal objective... not merely a localized or regional one.

For many Muslim leaders and extremists, patience and long-range thinking is huge. Islam has been around for 1400 years. Many Muslim

Chapter 2: The Present Situation

leaders and extremists have viewed themselves as one small part in the goal for Islam to become the world's faith, even by using force and manipulation. They have been content to use their lives to posture Islam for greater control years after they are dead and gone. Strengthened by their religious faith, they often spend years making promises from which they, or like-minded Muslims who will continue the cause after their deaths, will be content to walk away. This category of Muslims prepares themselves, or future like-minded Muslims, for the moment they have sure enough footing to make a significant jump in the amount of control they have over the non-believer.

This attribute of patience and long-range commitment to the ruling of Islam over all else can make it very difficult to recognize a Muslim leader's intentions. Is he seeking a position of power out of a degree of selflessness and the greater good, or with the intent to use manipulation and lies to weaken others and further Islamic control over the world? There are some signs that signal a manipulative Muslim leader's intentions. Unfortunately, these signs are only visible to the non-Muslim after they have been placed in a position of vulnerability, which usually comes with a costly consequence. The signs can show up almost immediately, but sometimes they can take years to surface.

Some examples of these signs, which you may have seen in the news, include the stories where cease-fires are broken or where peace treaties are disregarded. They include times when one Muslim organization is armed so it can fight against another Muslim organization, only to turn against those who armed them years later. It includes stories where Muslim organizations have pleaded for humanitarian aid and resources, only to divert much of what they received to further their Islamic cause in a militant way. It includes the stories where peaceful Muslims demanded to be given the right to govern themselves under SHARIA LAW in a non-Muslim country to the extent that it eventually threatens the right of the parent country to have differing values in the way it conducts itself politically and diplomatically.

Muslim leaders, who have ill intent toward non-Muslims, understand how non-Muslims think. Unfortunately, the reverse is not so true. Intolerant Muslim leaders and extremists know that the way to bog down the will of those who lack any kind of deep faith in God is by saying that they are being mistreated. They accuse their enemies of misdeeds. Sometimes their enemies have conducted themselves inappropriately. However, intolerant Muslim leaders and extremists are permitted by their faith to accuse their enemies of misdeeds even when it is a lie or after they have blatantly displayed the signs we just discussed. While the non-Muslim politicians and media scramble to "find the truth," the extremist's goals are being met: they are posturing themselves to gain, or regain, a position of strength through deception in accordance with their interpretations of the Qur'an and Hadith. When they feel that has been achieved, they will continue their efforts to spread Islam by force or simply to weaken their enemy until eventually he can be defeated, converted or killed.

The challenges we've touched on prevent any form of a lasting *political* solution to the Middle East crisis. For some of these challenges to be overcome, so that a long-term political solution could be attained, intolerant Muslims would have to reinterpret their beliefs. This is not likely to happen.

A Christian Perspective on These Problems

The Muslim extremist is willing to lose his life to kill his enemy. Jesus gave His life so that *even they* might change and enter into a relationship with Him.

As Christians, we are challenged to be Christ-like. Jesus taught us not to judge, but to leave judgment to Him. The challenges we looked at in this section are not intended to cause Christians to be afraid or to be judgmental against Muslims. The point is to be aware. The point is to be knowledgeable about how many Muslim leaders and extremists function so that we are not confused when we see our own country's leadership foundering and stumbling in their dealings with them. The point is to be "wise as a serpent and harmless as doves" (Matthew 10:16). Because there is no Christian country on the planet, as Christians we are living in a world full of darkness. Let us not be surprised, full of complaint, or full of worry and despair when others are stumbling around in that darkness. We must acknowledge and

Chapter 2: The Present Situation

understand the problems, but we must put our efforts into reflecting the light and love of Christ. And when it comes time for us to vote, let's fulfill our responsibilities as Christian citizens and vote well.

Jesus challenged us, as His followers, to love our enemies and to pray for them. Don't slip into spiritual complacency when Muslim leadership is not in a position of strength and so are tolerant and patient toward those who do not believe as they do. Be prepared for when that changes. We must remember to be Christ-like in all situations. We must remember that Pilate only had power because The Father permitted him to have it for a while.

As Christians we need to remain informed about what political decisions are being made in the name of our country. Being aware of what our government and politicians are saying is important. However, it is more important that we think and function as Christians first. As with Abraham, Jacob, Pharaoh, Israel and the Christian Church, etc. (pages 16, 19, 20, 25, 27, 31, 37, 40, 45, 58), this requires discernment. Discerning how God would handle through us whatever problem we might face requires us to turn away from our old patterns and let Him grow and mold us in our new selves in Christ. This, in turn, requires us to discern from the Spirit what our old patterns are. It includes being aware of our personal history in our own trials, i.e., the patterns by which our old selves would function and by which we are tempted. It also includes our history as Christians, both the good and the bad, particularly in light of the teachings and way of Christ. Being aware of our religious history is an important part in assisting us in not repeating Christianity's past mistakes.

Perspectives on Christian Religious Roots

What do we mean by our religious history as Christians? We are talking about the behavior of Christians throughout time. This isn't just about what we read in the Old and New Testaments, but also includes the time Christians occupied the Promised Land (page 49) and killed Jews and Muslims (page 59). It is important to remember that just as Sunnis and Shiites often discriminate and fight each other, Protestants and Catholics once did the same things. Just as some Islamic peoples carry their faith to extremes to justify killing and dominating others, so too Christians in the new world that became America once did the same. Christians once supported the killing and displacement of Native Americans. The same distortion of the Bible's teachings also supported slavery in America for a very long time.

As Christians, when we think in terms of our religious historical roots, most of us usually have some denomination with which we affiliate. But beyond that, the everyday Christian's sense of spiritual or religious history and roots tends to skip over 2000 years of history of how Christians have functioned. The everyday Christian's sense of spiritual or religious history and roots tends to jump from a person's denomination straight to the person of Jesus Christ. Some Christians recognize the importance of God's promises to Abraham. And often their sense of Christian history skips from Christ, over the entire Jewish nation and the bulk of the Old Testament, back to Abraham.

To both the practicing Jew and Muslim, this kind of perspective is rather like "spiritual hopscotch." Like the game children play by hopping over certain squares drawn on the sidewalk; one skips over the undesirable parts of history as if they didn't happen, or as if one is not connected to them. The Muslim view is that Christians can't claim to be the spiritual descendants of Abraham without also claiming the heritage of what Christians have done throughout time.

Remembering our Christian religious roots isn't about being able to recite the history of Christianity. It is about remembering that, while we are saved, we can't afford to be often unaware of the Holy Spirit pointing to how we are tempted to sin in our many trials. It means that while we are individuals, we are also to conduct ourselves as a universal Body of Christ. So, we can't afford to fail to discern when we are functioning like the Corinthians. We can't afford to fail to discern when we are being like Jonah. We can't afford to fail to discern when, like Abraham, we are tempted to take things into our own hands because we have the power to do so. As Christians, when we lack a godly remembering in these ways, it weakens our position in dealing with Muslims who function first based on their views of their faith. Most importantly, the failure to be aware of our own religious roots weakens a Christian's responsibility to figure out the implications of

Chapter 2: The Present Situation

how Christ and the Holy Spirit of God are to lead and control our problem-solving processes as followers of Christ.

When, as Christians, we are failing to view and respond to events in the world according to the actual teachings of our own faith in Christ, we will *tend* to align ourselves with politicians seeking to create external peace through political solutions. It will NOT be peace reflecting the peace of Christ (Colossians 3:15), so don't be surprised when the external peace doesn't last. As Christian people and as a Christian Body, when we place our hope in political solutions to resolve conflicts, then we will function in a fractured and ineffective way, becoming divided significantly along political lines, just as the Church did c. 1000 A.D. (page 57).

This is not to say that Christians always function this way. For example, on issues like abortion, marriage or feeding the poor we might tend to function more similarly according to our understanding of the teachings of Christ. However, when it comes to many kinds of conflicts, like those we see in the Middle East and the kinds we even experience with fellow believers, we often do not function in the ways of which Christ spoke. When we have conflicts with people we don't like, we often don't let Christ live through us and handle things His way. Many times we just give the person we don't like the silent treatment while secretly holding a grudge. This is no less sinful than the extremist who chooses to kill people he doesn't like. There are no acceptable degrees of sin. When a Christian forgets this, he will not discern the guidance of the Holy Spirit on how to follow Christ in his personal conflicts (which are spiritual battles) any better than the Muslim involved in a gun-toting holy war.

The bottom line is, if we function as Christians, most Muslims still may not be happy with us. However, at least Christ and our faith will guide more Christians' real-life decision-making, as opposed to many of us Christians functioning out of economic and political interest first, while being satisfied with just attending church.

MORE ABOUT HOW MUSLIMS, CHRISTIANS AND JEWS RELATE

In general, Muslims recognize that they have a certain relationship with Jews and Christians. Muslims consider Jews and Christians as having accepted previous (though superseded) revelations of God. Those previous, superseded versions were the Tanakh (Hebrew "Bible") and the Christian Bible. To the Muslims, each of these was superseded by the Qur'an. Islam actually accepts that some portions of the Tanakh and the Christian Bible are accurate. But in the Muslim mind, the current versions of the Tanakh and the Christian Bible are not completely true. Muslims view Jewish and Christian Scriptures as having been tainted through sinful living and inaccurate translation over time. To the Muslims, there are no existing Jewish and Christian Scriptures that are the accurate versions once given by God. This is why Muslims believe that God gave the Qur'an. It is considered the corrected version of God's Truth.

As the "Last Prophet," Muhammad saw himself as the last in a particular line of PROPHETS, starting with Adam and including Moses, Abraham, Ishmael, Jesus, etc. Being part of that line enabled Muhammad to "condemn" his own. Muhammad felt he was able to condemn the Christian and Jew in the sense that the Muslim, Jew and Christian all "believe in the same God." Muhammad's condemnation of the Jew and Christian was, to him, an "insider's" condemnation, as opposed to being an "outsider" to the Christian and Jew.

Tolerance Between Jews, Christians and Muslims

Because of these connections, Muslims refer to Christians and Jews as "People of the Book;" the Book being a general reference to the Jewish and Christian beliefs in their respective Scriptures. As such, Muslims can sometimes tolerate Christians and Jews as long as Islam is in control and the Christians and Jews do not seek to propagate their faiths. Muslim leadership and extremists often believe that if they are in a position to prevent it, they cannot allow Christians to evangelize because Christianity is a false faith.

Chapter 2: The Present Situation

Practicing Jews can sometimes tolerate living under this Islamic requirement because the Jewish faith does not focus on converting others to Judaism. In this sense, it is almost like Jews are really a "non-player" in teaching others to let God live through them. Their focus is on themselves as God's chosen people, not as a priesthood to the world as God called them to be. However, because of Islamic extremists, who seek to eradicate or oust from the lands of Israel the practicing Jews and peoples of Jewish descent, Jews are often drawn into conflict with Muslims.** This conflict arises in spite of the fundamental Islamic perspective of Muslim-Jewish religious connections.

Like the Jews, Christians in America can often tolerate Muslims, so long as the Muslims are not trying to control the religions of others. Christians can often tolerate Muslims so long as Christians (and peoples of other religions) are allowed to share their faith freely.

<u>Why "Good Muslims" Don't Take Care of
Changing the "Bad Muslims"</u>

As we mentioned earlier, fundamentally many Muslims can relate positively to Christians and practicing Jews. But, there are Muslims who can't or won't. These are often the Islamic extremists, but intolerance is also found under the national leadership of various Muslim denominations. In Muslim-controlled regions, it is not uncommon that Muslims are almost always opposed to anyone seeking to encourage a Muslim to convert to any other faith. The same charge is true among *some* Christians and practicing Jews.

So why don't the "good Muslims," who are more tolerant toward others make an effort to police or fight to control the intolerant "bad Muslims" and extremists?

When Islamic leaders and extremists take to fighting others and one another, they have the power and the guns. Most people are naturally

---

** Remember, the majority of the people who live in Israel today are of **Jewish descent**. This does NOT mean they are *practicing Jews* or that they believe God is the ultimate authority for their country's decision-making processes as did their forefathers Abraham, Isaac, Jacob, Moses, David, the Prophets, etc.

afraid of that. Just as people in a community with gangs are afraid and try to live "under the radar," so the "good Muslims" do the same. In many cities of the U.S. where there are gangs and violence, people remain there because they can't afford to go anywhere else. We don't see our citizens rising up in arms, even when they feel the police aren't doing a good job. It is usually no different for the average Muslim citizen in the Middle East.

In the West, we don't see large-scale uprisings of Christians seeking to "rein in" other Christians who have radical views about Christianity! While one Christian may view another as living by false doctrines, we don't see mainstream churches and groups investing huge amounts of efforts or resources to quell or eliminate the Christians who are spreading the "wrong beliefs."

The only reason it would cross our mind for one Muslim denomination to police another is because we are being affected and we don't like it. So while we might see the significance of our Christian religious roots and origins with respect to another's Christian views, or with respect to practicing Jews and Muslims, that knowledge doesn't make all the answers and solutions to the Middle East crisis immediately apparent. Though we have looked at an overview of the Jewish, Christian and Muslim histories in the unfolding of the Middle East crisis (Chapter 1), the crisis itself still can seem distant to us as Christians.

With this in mind, there are a couple important questions to answer.
- Are we more related to the Middle East crisis than we think?
- Is there a solution to the Middle East crisis?

While Jews, Christians and Muslims have different answers for these questions, in the next chapter we are going to look at some answers from a Christian-based perspective.

The short answers to the above questions are that we *are* related to the crisis more than it seems. And, there is a possible solution to the Middle East crisis. However, like we saw in the *Key Spiritual Battles* (featured in Chapter 1, pages 16, 19, 20, 25, 27, 31, 37, 40, 45, 58), the solution probably isn't going to look like what we'd expect externally!

Chapter 2: The Present Situation

Chapter 3: Crisis To Solution

The Middle East Crisis Is Similar To Everyone's Spiritual Crises

Behind the external fighting and suffering, essentially, the Middle East crisis is essentially one large scale example of spiritual crises (trials) involving even nations and peoples of different cultures. Even if we aren't in the Middle East, we too experience spiritual crises. Everyone on the planet experiences spiritual battles because everyone on the planet was born into the spiritual war.

When we are in a spiritual battle, it is not always easy, even for Christians, to hear or discern God even though He is trying to guide, comfort and correct us,. Part of the reason Jesus advised us not to judge one another is because accepting correction and change isn't always easy for us (Matthew 7:1-5). Why conduct ourselves as if we are masters of being corrected and changed by judging someone else when they might be struggling with a similar spiritual challenge?

While change is always a part of dealing with a trial or crisis, we often act as if it should be easy for someone else to accept whatever change we think God would have for them! When we in the West think of "those people" in the Middle East, we can probably come up with a list of changes we think they should willingly embrace.

To get an idea of how hard it might be for individuals in the Middle East to recognize God's solutions and corrections to them, it helps to see similar challenges to our own lives.

1. We have conflicts with others…
    a. … in our nation.
    b. … between denominations.
    c. … within our own churches.
    d. … with our neighbors.
    e. … within our extended families.

Chapter 3: Crisis To Solution

God is not the sponsor of conflicts in these areas of our lives! Do we think we are always right? If not, how are we letting God change us in order to eliminate our part of these conflicts? Christ indicated it would not be uncommon for biological families to grow apart from each other when some lived for Him and the others did not (Luke 12:51-53). So, how often do we correctly discern how God wants to change us when sensitive issues arise within the family? How often do we experience the peace of Christ amidst these kinds of troubles?

2. We also have conflict within our homes:
    a. Husband says, "I am the head of my home! I make the final decision!"
    b. Wife says, "I am equal before God! I get a say in all decisions!"
    c. Young Adult says, "I am on my own! I don't have to listen to you!"
    d. Teen says, "I am old enough to make my own decisions! I am not a child!"
    e. Child says, "My friends have one! Why don't I?"

When we look across the broad spectrum of Christian families, how well are we trained to seek out how God is trying to grow and change us more into His image? How quickly do we jump in response to the God of peace such that we let Him change our worldly desires?

3. We have conflict within ourselves:
    a. We think, "My time is too limited to be more involved in church!"
    b. We think, "My ministry is taking care of my family!"
    c. We think, "God doesn't want me or my family to be disadvantaged in life!"
    d. We think, "I handle issues in my marriage the way God wants me to!"
    e. We think, "The amount of time I introspect, pray and read the Bible is enough!"

When we are honest with ourselves, in terms of the external and internal conflicts we face, we can realize that we aren't always responsive followers of God. While as Christians we believe God forgives us for the sinfulness of our ways, we sometimes lack a bit of "keeping the pressure on ourselves" to make a more urgent effort to submit our freewill to His leading.

Of course, there are those that are often too hard on themselves, but many of us aren't hard enough. Sometimes we can get to a point in our lives where we act as if living for God is more about maintaining than deepening. Maintaining is not growing. Maintaining is a form of "spiritual retirement," which is not a godly concept spoken of in Scripture. Besides, many believers are often overwhelmed and swamped by the intricacies of their own life trials!

We sometimes forget that "running a good race" (1 Corinthians 9:24-27) isn't happening when we are stuck in our routine comfort zone or trying to simply survive our life issues. Sometimes this can happen without our realizing it. It stems from errors in our thinking about ourselves, our walk with God, and His attempts to get us to hear what He wants to change in us.

Christians know that the great commission is to make disciples of Christ (Matthew 28:19). Still, so many in the Body struggle with the fundamental aspects of how to be discipled by the Lord in their trials. Being discipled by God's Spirit goes far beyond church attendance, tithing, reading the Bible and praying for whatever we want. The stakes for change amongst the Middle Eastern peoples are as high as are the changes God seeks for Christians, who are, by lack of training, stuck in such minimalist Christianity. If many *Christians* struggle to get this, how much more difficult might it be for others to discern and cooperate with changes God seeks in them? It is important that we understand this.

MISPERCEPTIONS OF GOD AND OURSELVES FUEL CRISIS

Regardless whether a person is a Christian, Jew or Muslim, any misperceptions one has of God or oneself, in terms of how we are actually functioning in relationship to God, will create and perpetuate crises. We will experience crises of our own making and in our

Chapter 3: Crisis To Solution

relationships with others. Fundamentally, this is because we act upon untruth, i.e., that which God is not, whenever our perceptions of God are off.

Below are some questions we often don't really think about unless somebody directly asks us a question. When we don't think about our answers to certain questions like these, we live our lives with unnoticed and unexpressed assumptions. Not good. It helps if we ask introspective questions of ourselves and what we believe, then figure out our answers and evaluate whether those answers are really the ones by which we ought to live. When we determine our answers may not be satisfactory before God, we can expect that God is probably trying to tell us to do something about it!

1. What kind of god is God?
    a. Is He an angry/punishing God Who wants me to act only out of duty and fear?
    b. Is He a loving/excusing God Who doesn't expect me to change in uncomfortable ways?
    c. Is He a loving/correcting/guiding God Who attempts to use my life trials to assist me to change, grow, and mature?

2. How accurate are my core beliefs?
    a. Completely correct.
    b. Mostly correct.
    c. Correct enough.

3. How well do I apply my beliefs to my trials and follow God's guidance?
    1. All the time.
    2. Whenever I can figure it out.
    3. Sometimes I can't figure it out, so I just do the best I can.

A person's answers to these questions can assist in creating a sense of urgency to seek out growth in what one believes and how one approaches life. When our truth doesn't match God's truth, it limits our relationship with him, and with others. When we live according to a truth that is, from God's perspective, wrong, God is trying to tell us about it, but we have to discern this with our hearts and seek out His answers wholeheartedly.

WHAT HAPPENS WHEN WE ARE WRONG?

Self-assessment, evaluation and introspection are vital to discerning whether our understanding of God and His expectations for us are correct. This discernment must be done on an individual basis. It is vital to God opening our spiritual eyes and ears. It starts by asking ourselves, "How do I recognize God's solutions to my misperceptions?" In other words, we can ask ourselves, "If I am wrong about some of my beliefs, or if I'm lacking in following God's lead in my life, could I really hear God tell me specifically how to change?"

Can I hear God tell me...
1. ...when my beliefs are incorrect?
2. ...if and when I can't agree with others when they tell me that my beliefs are wrong?
3. ...when some of my actions are not based on the beliefs I have which are true?

HOW DOES GOD SEEK TO COMMUNICATE SOLUTIONS TO EVERY PERSON?

When it comes to trying to "hear God," this is called *discernment*. There are basically two ways God tries to communicate to us, so that we can discern whatever changes He might want to make in us.

1. Through His written Word.
2. By speaking to our hearts.

Both of the above must work together. The first is not a substitute for the second. While the first is hugely important, it does not automatically lead to the second.

While as Christians we do believe that the Christian Bible is the inerrant Word of God, we often make assumptions about how we are to go about discerning God's solutions and corrections for us. We will look at these assumptions next. If, as Christians, we have such errant assumptions, then how much more difficult would it be for others (like militant Muslims) to see the errors of their assumptions, especially when they have a very different faith system?

MYTHS ABOUT HEARING/EMBRACING GOD'S SOLUTIONS

When it comes to discerning and embracing God's changes in us personally, there are some things we sometimes say or think. Some of these are very inaccurate. Here are some examples:

Myth 1.   God made me the way I am.

> Matthew 26:24-25. God certainly didn't make Judas Iscariot the way he was... Satan played a big part in that! The quirks, preferences, opinions and behaviors we sometimes have might be "normal" when we look around at others in society. However, in terms of the spiritual war, some of them may have been developed throughout our lives as a result of Satan's often hidden influence.

> It is true that each of us has gifts that God has given us for the purpose of building and contributing to the work of the Body of Christ. However, Satan's self-appointed role is to get us to use them in ways that satisfy our sin nature while claiming to be contributing to the work of the Lord. Satan's temptations often create friction or non-cooperation within the Body of Christ when it comes to gifts. Judas Iscariot was a finance guy. Perhaps he would have claimed that his gift was working with money, finances, etc. Maybe that was true. But as we see, just

because it might have been his "gift," that didn't prevent Satan from tempting him to use it in ungodly ways. You may want to look at Judas' confusion over how to spend money in God's service in John 12:1-8.

Myth 2.   God will always change the desires in me that don't serve Him.

1 Kings 11:1-6. When King Solomon had the desire to marry many women in order to create peace for the nation of Israel, God did not give him that desire, and God certainly didn't change it automatically. Like King Solomon, we too have freewill, which includes the responsibility to evaluate all of our desires and to discern from God when they are not "of God." This is true whether society and culture say certain of our desires are "OK" or "normal." It is very difficult to discern God's corrections when we aren't well trained to discern our old self's desires.

Myth 3.   God will make me feel bad about things I believe, if my belief is wrong.

Acts 5:1-10. When Ananias and Sapphira were thinking about keeping some of the money for themselves, they might have been thinking that God would want them to take a common sense approach to their future financial security and retirement. Who knows what they were thinking. Whatever it was, it made sense to them, and they did not feel bad about doing what they did – and they had even discerned the guidance of God's Spirit to them! The lesson is that God will not always make us feel bad about our beliefs if we let ourselves become skilled at distracting ourselves from or ignoring our hearts. Godly introspection is a responsibility we all have… it is part of "carrying our cross."

Myth 4.   God will always show me from the Bible whether I should do a thing or not.

(Acts 10:25-29). When Peter felt God wanted him to go to the home of a Gentile (a Roman centurion); Peter did not get that direction from the Bible. In fact, the Scriptures he had at the time (the Old Testament) actually forbade such an action!

Part of following the Lord means we are going to experience situations in which the answers we find are corroborated by whether or not our hearts are experiencing the peace of Christ concerning something we think might be God's guidance. Discerning God's guidance in some crises, conflicts and trials can only be done by double-checking that the desire of our heart is only about fulfilling His desire, especially when doing so puts us in an awkward spot!

Myth 5.   I will always hear God if He is trying to tell me that I'm believing something to be "true" when it isn't. (Corinthian Christians)

1 Corinthians 5:1-5. Just because we are followers of Christ doesn't mean that we will automatically hear or discern when God is trying to correct us. If this were not the case, many of the New Testament letters would not have been written in an attempt to set things straight with believers who were "off track." Paul's letter to the Christians at Corinth is a perfect example. While the recipients of the letter were Christians, they were tuning out the Spirit of God within! Discerning the guidance and correction of God's Spirit not only requires a desire to do so, but requires the application of the Bible's principles for listening to God.

Myth 6.   God does not ask me to do something that isn't natural to the way He made me. (Abraham)

Genesis 22:1-3. We tend to think that God will not ask us to do things that go against our grain. However, many stories in the Bible show that God *does* often want us to do things that are well out of our comfort zone. Being able to discern God's voice in our hearts, when He is telling us to do something that is "not normal," is not a skill that comes automatically to us. We have to let God cultivate this kind of discernment in us by truly practicing the process of putting His will before our own. This requires being Biblically trained in how to be discipled by God's invisible Spirit to follow Christ in real-life trials. It also involves caring less about what we want the outcome of our trials to be, and being more at peace while leaving the outcome to the Lord, and this isn't about being passive or inactive!

While God told Abraham to sacrifice his son Isaac; God ultimately prevented Abraham from doing so. This does not mean that God will always do the same for us (Hebrews 11:35-40). After all, God expected Abraham to wait 25 years for the promise of a son to be fulfilled… that length of time is probably out of most people's comfort zone when it comes to fulfilling our "good" desires. If we knew someone who had waited for "God's will" to be accomplished and it was taking longer than a year, most people would tend to think that the person "heard God wrong." We tend to expect immediate results from God. This is where giving the outcome to Him comes in to play.

Chapter 3: Crisis To Solution

HEARING/DISCERNING GOD'S SOLUTIONS (CHRISTIAN PERSPECTIVE)

Hearing, or discerning, God's solutions for us personally on a consistent basis starts by entering into a relationship with Him. But again, just because we do this does not mean that we will automatically discern God's guidance to us on a consistent basis. This truth is demonstrated in the many of the situations examined from the Bible in the *Key Spiritual Battles* feature of this book (pages 16, 19, 20, 25, 27, 31, 37, 40, 45, 58).

There are some fundamental principles that the Bible speaks to when it comes to discerning God's guidance on how to deal with conflict, wherever we might find it. Discernment involves letting God grow us, not just in our knowledge of the Bible and of God, but also in terms of how well we give our decision-making to the Lord in our trials. Both individually and as a Body of believers, how can we expect those in the Middle East to discern God's guidance to them when, as disciples of Christ and members of a royal priesthood, we often do not or cannot do the same in our own trials? As Christians, who are a part of the Body of Christ, how can we expect to function as a "royal priesthood" to the world, including the Middle East, if, as a collective Body, so many believers in our churches are struggling to discern God's guidance to them in their own daily lives?

Sending missionaries to witness to the peoples of the Middle East is part of the solution to introduce the message and peace of Christ to that region of the world. But, on its own, it is not enough. Another vital part of introducing the peace of Christ anywhere in the world hinges on discipleship at home. It hangs on teaching believers *how* to be discipled by the Lord in their personal lives. It is the essence of teaching believers how to be led by God's Holy Spirit within. This is life changing. It is a super critical portion of following completely through the process of making disciples of Christ (Matthew 28:19).

Trials are a spiritually normal part of the most basic context in which all humanity exists: the spiritual war. Because of this, part of being grown during trials involves discerning how we are tempted during trials. While from God's perspective our old self is dead in Christ, from an experiential standpoint the temptation(s) associated with a given trial appeals to part of us, the part which the Bible says is our old self (or fleshly self). This is where discernment in a trial starts: seeking to discern our old self desires and the temptation which we are being presented in the trial. Discerning old desires and temptation in ourselves is essential to overcoming them in Christ and letting Him live through us. These are practical, foundational Biblical principles when it comes to "being discipled" by the Lord in everyday living.

Learning to be discipled by the Lord in our lives starts with…
1. …entering into a relationship with God (John 3:16). This is where discipleship begins. Some of discipleship in the **basics** of Christ is discussed in Hebrews 6:1-2. Being discipled ***beyond*** those basics involves…

2. …growing in discernment and the practical side of walking with the Lord (Philippians 1:9-11).
   This includes:
   a. Connecting with a local Body of believers (Hebrews 10:23-25).
   b. Learning how to discern how you are tempted in a trial (Romans 6:12, Ephesians 4:22-24, James 1:14-15).
   c. Learning how to discern God's correction during trials (Hebrews 12:4-6). This is related to learning what it means to keep pace with the Spirit's guidance in your life (Galatians 5:25).
   b. Letting peace rule in your heart, even in trials (Colossians 3:15). When your heart isn't at peace, learn to discern what God seeks to change in you so you can be at peace.
   c. Prayer is a vital part of a Christian's connection to God. The key to consistently praying prayers that are in alignment with God's will is the integral part in which discernment plays in the Christian life… even in terms of prayer.
      i. Prayer is not a carte blanche ticket to simply ask for whatever one desires when that desire could very well be part of a temptation (an exception to this might very well be a singular prayer by the desperate lost individual, which God might grant to demonstrate that

He is, in fact, present, listening, and looking for that one to come to Him).
ii. While there are many references to praying at all times in all situations and for what one desires, for the believer, the context of each of these is the proper guide to prayer as demonstrated in the Lord's Prayer in Matthew 6:9-13, particularly in verse 10, "...Your will be done on earth as it is in heaven...." This means that when we pray, it isn't about praying for what we want but for what God wants us to want – especially when our desires may be the result of being tempted in a trial before our hearts are able to discern God's guidance. It is imperative that our prayer reaches the point where our actual desire is for God's will to be done above ours – and that we are at peace with this.
1) This principle is again demonstrated in Jesus prayer in the Garden of Gethsemane, "...My Father, if this cannot pass away unless I drink it, Your will be done" (Matthew 26:42).
2) As believers, only when we pray that HIS will be done over a worldly desire of ours can we expect for those prayers to be answered in accordance with Matthew 21:22. How can we expect a particular prayer to be answered if it is from a heart that, in that trial, has fallen into desiring something that evil has lured us to desire (James 1:13-15)?
3. The above are just a couple Biblical concepts that are important to helping us learn how to submit to the Lord in trials so that He can open our spiritual eyes and ears (Mark 8:17-18).

With these things in mind, let's conclude by looking at some possible solutions to the Middle East crisis.

POSSIBLE SOLUTIONS

Solution 1: A first solution is that, as Christians, we trust the Middle East crisis resolution finding to the politicians, diplomats and military hoping they will be successful. We could continue to view the Middle East crisis as a crisis that "those people" in Middle East have, which sometimes affects us directly. We can continue to try to solve the crisis politically, by trying to figure out how to best get along with "those people," and how to get "those people" to get along with each other. This solution has resulted in a few temporary successes over the last 40-50 years. While this solution has its merits, it is important to realize that it will never produce more than temporary results.

Solution 2: A second solution is that, as Christians, we embrace Solution 1 (above) while basically believing nothing will really ever change "over there in the Middle East" until God is ready to bring this world to an end. The Jew, the Christian, and the Muslim each hold beliefs in terms of the concept that God will eventually bring this world to an end. Looking forward to that end is often a deeply held view that can inadvertently cause us to conduct ourselves as if there is nothing we really must do to let Christ change us more before the end comes. This kind of perspective can make it easier to slip into functioning as if we, personally, have embraced most of the changes that God would make in our lives, particularly in terms of dealing with conflict and crisis. This perspective is dangerous for the individual follower of Christ and the Body... it facilitates living in this world and actually being of it, but without realizing how that is happening.

Solution 3: A third solution is that, as individual believers and as a Body of Christ, we work on getting better at letting Christ live through us according to the Biblical concept of being in the world while not being of it. This means we indirectly address the Middle East crisis by directly improving how we deal with any form of crisis and conflict in our own lives. Wherever we encounter crisis or conflict, the goal is to serve the Lord's purpose of impacting the world, by learning how to let the Lord be in charge of our decision-making. This is living God's written Word.

Peoples of all races and nationalities are simply trying to make it through life. Every Christian's life must demonstrate and reflect that a

Chapter 3: Crisis To Solution

healthy relationship with Christ involves discerning how He is trying to lead each step of our lives, not just by praying to the Lord, but by being able to actively discern His Holy Spirit's counsel to us concerning our problem-solving. In short, we have to be able to listen with our hearts! This does not come to us automatically just because we believe in Christ. It involves embracing how God continually seeks to change us personally.

Everybody is trying to figure out how to handle their problems without inadvertently creating more! As Christians are discipled to discern the Holy Spirit's guidance in how to follow Christ with our own worries, concerns and fears, our lives will be substantially filled with more peace. This is one of the things that is supposed to be unique about Christians. As more Christians learn to live the Bible's teachings on spiritual problem-solving in real-life situations, our lives will attract the attention of others who experience the unsatisfactory results of leaning on one's own ideas of how to respond to life's concerns. The ability to handle conflicts in a Christ-like way will generate more involvement in the Church. (Involvement in the Church isn't supposed to be limited to stay-at-home moms or dads, the financially stable, the retired, or for those called to be in some Church leadership position.) Being discipled in how to let God lead our decision-making creates productive believers in the Church. It creates time in Christians' lives to minister to others and to serve in the building up of the Body. It can bring more creativity, flexibility, service and unity to the Body like we haven't seen since 1st Century Christianity.

The Middle East crisis cannot be solved by nations because it requires individuals to change how they make decisions. Individual decision-making will not change unless it is Christ-led. The Middle East crisis, along with all other crises, can be influenced for the better by individuals under the direction of the Holy Spirit, Whom Christ secured for His followers (John 14:15-17, 16:7-15). This doesn't mean that nations should quit trying to find a solution. Actually, at this point in this book we aren't trying to focus on what nations should or shouldn't do. We are focusing on the "spiritual nation" of believers in Christ. Wherever each individual believer is, he or she must be capable of addressing each crisis and problem he or she faces as the Lord directs through His Spirit. In this way the Body of Christ can function as a blessing to the world – an extension of God's second promise to Abraham from a Christian perspective. The more that Christians are discipled to discern God's guidance in their own conflicts, the less chaos those conflicts will generate. The more the peace of Christ will abound through us in this world.

If you can't see how God could use this solution to impact the Middle East crisis, realize that it hinges on the Christian world's ability to hear God trying to lead us, individually and as a Body, during crises. Our role as followers of Christ is to let Him deal with crisis and conflict through us (Galatians 2:20). Perhaps the more we cooperate with Him, the more He can work through us to resolve conflicts elsewhere in the world. This solution, Solution 3, is the solution on which we will focus from this point to the end of the book.

The Holy Spirit's Role in Resolving any Conflict or Crisis

A key to implementing this 3rd Solution includes reframing our views of the role and place of the Holy Spirit in the Christian walk. The role of the Spirit is greater than just providing us inspiration. It is more than a nebulous background-role in our lives. The Holy Spirit's role is more than dispensing spiritual gifts among believers. The Holy Spirit was given to us so that in every problem and issue we face He would attempt to "teach us all things" (John 14:26). He seeks to teach us all things we need to learn in order to allow Christ to live through us in each and every problem, worry and conflict in our own lives, as they occur in real time! The Holy Spirit seeks to show us how God is trying to grow us in our trials, and how to experience the love of Christ *during* our problems and issues.

Our part in our relationship with God is to incline our hearts to Him during a crisis so we can hear His Spirit with our heart. This requires us to let the Lord change and grow us. While we might understand this concept mentally, a refreshed emphasis on being discipled is needed.

Chapter 3: Crisis To Solution

Leading people to a relationship with Christ is just the start. It is vital that the Christian community get stronger in making disciples who are capable of discerning how God is literally trying to lead their decision-making and problem-solving processes concerning their unique, real-world problems. The Israelites were looking forward to the Messiah, yet they couldn't see Him standing in front of them. So, they leaned on their own understanding while praying for the Messiah. Similarly, we can slip into leaning on our own understanding while praying to God for help and guidance. The Spirit is attempting to teach us, but many of us Christians aren't trained in how to listen. When this happens in a Christian's life, it reflects a lack of discipleship that goes beyond the elementary teachings of a relationship with Christ (Hebrews 6:1-2).

If there is to be a solution to the Middle East crisis, then Christianity's part will involve, in some large part, embracing discipleship that goes beyond the basics to address the root of the problem...

> **...crisis and conflict itself, wherever it is ineffectively addressed, becomes a weapon used by the spiritual forces at work against God Himself.**

Solution 3 centers on the concept that conflict, wherever it arises, is not of the Lord but is fueled by all things which are against God. God is not a God of disorder or confusion (1 Corinthians 14:33). Conflict and real-life problems are the context in which we are being baited and lured into leaning on our own creative problem-solving techniques. This is the kind of thinking and decision-making that perpetuates conflict without intending to do so! While God will always seek to grow us through conflict, the idea is to be able to discern and follow His Spirit in us (Galatians 5:25).

> **The standard for knowing when we have properly discerned and are following the Lord's lead in response to a crisis or conflict is that we will have peace *during* the trial, not just when it is over. (John 14:27; Colossians 3:12-15)**

The idea is to be centered in Christ and His peace in the midst of our life storms. This is different from enduring conflict, not being certain of how God would have us respond to crisis, or only being able to experience peace and spiritual comfort after a crisis comes to a conclusion. The role of God's Spirit is to lead Christians beyond this on a regular basis.

Living in the world, yet not being of it, involves "waging war, but not as the world wages war" (2 Corinthians 10:3-4). It involves direct, practical interaction with God's Spirit in how to let the person of Christ lead in our life issues. It involves understanding our roles, in Christ, as those roles pertain to our families, to our work, and within the Body. It involves understanding and respecting the influential role God's Spirit seeks to have in our decision-making.

Once we have a better idea of the Holy Spirit's role in our relationship with Christ, there are still some other challenges that will require us to examine our lives and to seek to grow more in them.

Challenges for Christians And Solution 3

Pray For Our Persecuted Christian Brothers And Sisters. This is essential. We must pray for their courage, and that they will experience a strong sense of the peace of Christ in trials, no matter how bad things get. We must pray for them because they could be in awful situations like those described in Hebrews 11:36-40. We must pray that they would let the light of Christ shine through them, even when their future in this world is uncertain. In part we must pray for their strength, but we must also remember to pray that we too stand stronger for Christ in our conflicts and life trials. We must pray so we remember the example in Hebrews 12:1-11, to which we must live.

Pray For Our Enemies And Those Who Do Evil. It is important that we pray not for their destruction, but that they would respond to God's Spirit. We must pray that those who are driven by hate and anger would become aware of the hole these untransformed feelings create in the heart... the hole that only Christ can fill. We must pray that those who are enemies of God's goodness and love discern their need for the peace of Christ. We must pray for our enemies with a thankful heart... thankful that their cause's gains can never be more than God will permit. We must pray that our strife with those who do evil would never lead us to fall to the temptation of letting our own hearts be filled with judgment over the love and peace of Christ.

Discernment Skills Are Essential For Any Believer To Function As An Effective Part Of A Royal Priesthood. God intended for the nation of Israel to function as a kingdom of priests to the world (Exodus 19:5-6). Israel has not yet embraced this role. God established a new covenant with the world so that through His Son He would raise up a royal priesthood and a holy people (1 Peter 2:9-12). This priesthood crosses all lines: geography, culture, family, language, religious background, societal status, financial status, and even life and death itself. As Christians, this is supposed to be us. While some Christians are functioning in this priesthood role, *some* is not satisfactory. The Church must return to discipleship, including teaching the Biblical "how to" of discerning God's guidance in real life. Christians, particularly new believers, must be discipled how to follow the Spirit's guidance in problem-solving... not based on emotion and feel-good moments, but from a heart centered in peace. This is vital to submitting to God as He seeks to grow ALL believers into this priesthood.

We Must Focus Less On How Dark It Is And Focus More On Spreading The Light. Let's stop being surprised every time we hear stories on the news on how much darker the world is becoming! When a nation's leaders are not actually following Christ, they will make poor decisions. This is how the world works. The Bible tells us this. Let's not become so wrapped up in talking about the ever-growing darkness that we lose valuable time in which we could discuss and seek more ways to be the light of the world!

There were many crises and political issues going on at the time the New Testament books were written. The Roman Senate was making decisions impacting Christians' quality of life. Slavery was permitted, and often Christians were slaves. Romans and Jews were persecuting Christians. Still, nowhere in the New Testament do we read recommendations on how a Roman citizen should vote in a Senatorial race! Nowhere do we read how Christians should seek to weigh in on various political issues. This doesn't mean they shouldn't or didn't.

This doesn't imply that as Christians we should not weigh in on issues; when it is time to vote, let's vote. The point is that living for Christ was the driving issue for 1st Century Christians, not politics.

We must pray for our leaders (Romans 13:1-7). Our leaders are accountable before God for their action and inaction. Still, though we will pray for them, let us not be surprised that they need our prayers.

In between our opportunities to vote, we ought to spend more of our Christian fellowshipping time discussing how to be the light on the hill. It means we ought to focus more on how to live the Bible's teachings and how to allow those teachings to govern and alter our perspective on dealing with problems we face in the world in a Christ-like manner. It means we ought to focus more on whether our lives are showing God's unique light to others!

Accept That Currently There Is No Christian Country On The Planet. Perhaps one of the reasons American Christians often discuss (at length) the ever-growing darkness of this world and of our leadership is because we grew up thinking that our country was a Christian country. We have to get past this. We need to reframe our thinking. Many non-Muslim countries (including America) are functioning the way they do *because* they are NOT Christian-based. Christians might do better to recognize that as of this publication, in 2014, no Christian in the world is living in a Christian country! There is NO country on the planet that is governing and making its policies specifically in the name of Christ.

What we read about in the New Testament is how to function in a country that is NOT Christian..., which is exactly the situation in the entire world, including America. What we see in the early centuries of Christianity is that the world did not change overnight. However, as each individual believer sought to live for the Lord, according to the guidance of God's Spirit and the written Word, the world was certainly changed! The world changed because large numbers of believers were taught how to discern and follow the Lord's guidance to them, through the Holy Spirit, regardless what kind of trial or conflict they face. The world changed because more believers were reflecting the light of God in their daily lives. As Christians, we must get back to this!

Chapter 3: Crisis To Solution

Some Christians Might Experience Earthly Prosperity; All Christians Must Be Discipled To Experience Spiritual Prosperity.
What greater measurement is there of spiritual prosperity than to experience the peace and the presence of the Lord *during* a trial, to know what temptation you are to avoid, to know how God is specifically trying to grow you in the trial, and to be completely certain and confident that you know how God wants you to respond to the trial?

In New Testament times, wherever Christians were mistreated or got the short end of the stick, we don't read in the Bible how they were to go about getting justice from their government. We don't read about how they were to go about getting vindication for wrongs done to them. What we read are teachings about how to have a strong sense of peace and fulfillment in Christ, regardless of the worldly circumstances which they experienced. What we read about is how to have more love and community within the Body. What we read about in the New Testament is how believers were encouraged and taught to discern the guidance of God's Spirit so as to respond in godly ways to issues and crises they faced in their non-Christian countries. This is the essence of prosperity in Christ (Hebrews 10:32-36).

A Final Consideration

As Christians, let's not just be educated on the religious origins of the Middle East crisis. Our prayer is that all the members of the Body of Christ will grow more strongly in discipleship and discernment so as to live the faith that we have in Christ Jesus.

For more information about being discipled *beyond* the basics, Biblical discernment, growing in trials and discovering God's guidance to you in any trial you face, the *Keys Series* book *Feelings 101: Pain to Peace, 2nd Edition* is a Bible-based, self-paced course oriented on helping you grow in these areas. See the information at the back of this book.

May the peace of Christ rule in your hearts....

APPENDIX 1: RELIGIOUS COMPOSITION OF NATIONS

The charts on the following page reflect how many people of which religion reside in selected countries.

These percentages do not reflect missionaries, diplomats, or visiting foreigners, but rather residents of a particular religion. So, for example, the number of Christians in Iraq in 1990 shows about 8% of the population. That number doesn't count Christians visiting Iraq from other countries. It means there are about 8% of the Iraqis who are actually claiming to be Christian.

For percentages of Christians, these percentages reflect all Christian denominations together.

YES = some residents in this country claim the faith indicated, but the exact numbers are not known.

NO = countries reported NO to any persons of this religion being permanent residents their country.

UNK = Unknown. According to Library of Congress Country Studies, CIA World Fact Book, or U.S. Department Background Notes, it is (was) not known whether or not any persons of this religion reside in the particular country. This uncertainty likely reflects the way that particular country conducts its census information gathering.

Appendix 1: Religious Composition Of Nations

As of 1990

	JEW	CHRISTIAN	SUNNI	SHIITE
ISRAEL	90%	YES	YES	NO
JORDAN	NO	YES	91%	YES
LEBANON	NO	YES	45%	45%
SYRIA	NO	YES	82%	YES
IRAN	YES	YES	5%	93%
IRAQ	NO	8%	40%	50%
KUWAIT	UNK	UNK	70%	30%
SAUDI ARABIA	UNK	UNK	95%	5%
BAHRAIN	UNK	YES	YES	YES

As of 2014

	JEW	CHRISTIAN	SUNNI	SHIITE
ISRAEL	75%	2%	17%	
JORDAN	YES	2%	95%	<2%
LEBANON	YES	40%	27%	27%
SYRIA	YES	10%	74%	13%
IRAN	<1%	<1%	10%	90%
IRAQ	<1%	<1%	37%	65%
KUWAIT	UNK	17%	77% (most Sunni)	
SAUDI ARABIA	YES	YES	85%	10%
BAHRAIN	<1%	14%	25%	60%
TURKEY	<1%	<1%	99.8 (most Sunni)	
ENGLAND	UNK	59%	4%	
SPAIN	UNK	94%	UNK	UNK
FRANCE	1%	85%	5-10%	
AMERICA	1%	77%	<1%	

APPENDIX 2: DEFINITIONS

NOTE: Words in *bold italics* can be cross-referenced within the definitions list below.

ABRAHAM (a.k.a. Abram): God made His three *promises* to Abraham. Abraham's wife was Sarah. Sarah was unable to have children. Abraham and Sarah were anxious to have one of God's promises fulfilled sooner than God wanted, i.e., that they would have a son. As a result, Sarah approached Abraham about sleeping with her Egyptian maidservant, *Hagar*. Abraham and Hagar had a son, *Ishmael*. Eventually, Sarah had a son, *Isaac*, with Abraham (Genesis 21:2-3).

Muhammad viewed God's three promises as being passed down to him through Ishmael. The *Jews* and *Christians* see God's three promises as being passed down through Isaac.

ABU BA'KR: After the death of *Muhammad*, Ba'Kr was accepted as the first *Caliph*, and most *Muslims* also accept Ba'Kr as the first *Imam*. Ba'Kr was a father-in-law to Muhammad. Muslims accepting Ba'Kr became known as *Sunni*. This distinguished the Sunnis from the *Shiites*, who accepted and followed *Ali ibn Abi Talib* (a.k.a., Ali). Ba'Kr said that the *Qur'an* is to be interpreted by a direct descendant of Muhammad.

AL-QAEDA: Literally "The Base." It is a *Sunni*, global militant *Islamic* organization founded by Osama bin Laden in the late 1980's in Pakistan. Its goal is to oppose laws of man in favor of strict *Sharia Law*. Al-Qaeda is considered a terrorist organization by the U. N. and most Western governments. Al-Qaeda believes it is religiously sanctioned to kill civilians, including liberal and non-Sunni *Muslims*. (also see footnote on page 66)

Appendix 2: Definitions

ALI IBN ABI TALIB (ALI): The cousin and son-in-law of *Muhammad*. Ali was the fourth *Caliph* (who was also the last of the Caliphs considered to have been "rightly guided" in the teachings of Muhammad). Ali was accepted by some *Muslims* after the death of Muhammad. These Muslims became known as *Shiites*. This distinguishes the Shiites from the *Sunnis*, who accepted and followed *Abu Ba'Kr*. Ali said that the *Qur'an* is to be interpreted by Muhammad's teaching and practice and does NOT have to be done by a direct descendant of Muhammad.

ALLAH: Literally "The God." The *Muslim* name for God. Allah is viewed by Muslims as the same God who spoke to *Abraham* and Jesus. Muslims believe that the God of Abraham, Isaac and Jacob gave certain revelations to *Muhammad*, which were put together to form the *Qur'an*. For more, see page 4.

AYATOLLAH: Literally "Sign of God." Among *Shiites*, an Ayatollah is a leader who is regarded as especially learned. Ayatollah Khomeini was recognized as "Vilayat Faqih of Supreme Temporal Representative in Iran of the Hidden *Imam*." This is how you can tell Ayatollah Khomeini was Shiite.

BIBLE, THE (CHRISTIAN): (see also page 7) The sacred writings of the *Christian* faith. The two divisions of the Bible are the Old and the New Testaments. The Old Testament in the Christian Bible is very similar to the *Jewish* sacred Scriptures, *Tanakh* – the Hebrew "Bible." The New Testament contains the record of *Jesus* and the guidelines for living the Christian faith based on a relationship with Him.

CALIPH (CALIPHATE): One of the successors of *Muhammad* who functions as temporal and spiritual head of the community and faith of *Islam*.

A Caliphate refers to a period of rule under a Caliph. Since the founding of Islam, there have been a number of Caliphates. The first Caliphate was the Rashidun Caliphate under which all of Islam was united (632-661 A.D.). Under the second Caliphate, the Umayyads Caliphate, Islam split into the *Sunni* and *Shiite* "denominations." Since then, the Caliphates have been mostly Sunni. The majority of Shiites are still waiting for the "Hidden *Imam*," who will establish a rightful continuation of a Caliphate when he returns.

CHRISTIAN, CHRISTIANITY: The religious faith whose adherents hold that *Jesus* is the physical incarnation of God, the Messiah promised in the *Jewish* Scriptures. By means of His death and resurrection, forgiveness of sin and a relationship with God becomes available to all people. The Old and New Testaments of the Christian *Bible* are the divine authority for religious belief and practice for Christians.

DISCERN, DISCERNMENT: "the quality of being able to (perceive), grasp and comprehend what is obscure (or concealed), to see or understand a difference; to detect; a power to see what is not evident to the average mind...."[8] In this book, we look at several key spiritual battles that show the importance of discernment to *Christians* and their ability to follow the Lord during trials (pages 16, 19, 20, 25, 27, 31, 37, 40, 45, 58). The *Bible* shows us that God's will often does not immediately occur to us because, in spiritual battles, we are being tempted and deceived (James 1:13-15). That deception stipulates the importance of discernment to walking with God during a trial. The ability to discern God's will in a trial involves a heart that is at peace and which changes in response to God's lead. Discernment involves not following one's own understanding or natural ways or attempting to resolve a trial in a manner that seems natural to us. For more about discernment in following Christ and His teachings in real-life situations, see the list of Scripture verses listed in the second paragraph of *MESSAGE OF CHRIST*, page 110.

DIVINE LAWS: The *Jews*, *Christians* and *Muslims* each believe in certain divine laws given from God. There are some overall similarities, but there are some significant differences too. For

---

[8]Merriam-Webster, I. (2003). *Merriam-Webster's collegiate dictionary.* Includes index. (Eleventh ed.). Springfield, Mass.: Merriam-Webster, Inc.

Appendix 2: Definitions

Jews – see the *Law*. For Christians – see *Message of Christ*. For Muslims – see *Sharia Law*.

DOME OF THE ROCK: see *Jerusalem*.

DRUZE: A denomination (sect) of *Shiites*, who believe that Hakim, the Sixth Fatimid *Caliph*, was the final representative of *Allah*. Their beliefs are drawn from *Judaism* and *Christianity*, as well as *Islam*. Druze is a closed, secretive, extremely religious and pacifist community.

EDOMITES: see *Esau*

ESAU: A son of *Isaac*. Brother of *Jacob*. Esau was the firstborn, but sold his birthright to his brother, Jacob. Esau's descendants became known as the Edomites (Genesis 36:9). There are several references to the Edomites in the Old Testament (and the *Tanakh*). The Edomites often fought with and even invaded lands occupied by the *Israelites*. When the Romans eventually conquered lands in the Middle East, the Edomites were among those conquered. The Romans called the Edomites, "Idumaea." When the Roman General *Titus* laid siege to and ultimately conquered *Jerusalem* in 70 A.D., the Idumaea (Edomites) were permitted to enter the city to rob and loot it. After this, the Edomites pretty much disappear from the history books. The assumption is that they ceased to exist as a people and were absorbed into other cultures.

FIVE PILLARS OF FAITH, THE: The five essentials of *Islam's* faith. Most of the Islamic sects or "denominations" hold to these, although they may disagree sharply on other issues.
- To believe in the One True God (*Allah*).
- To pray at the prescribed five times each day.
- To give alms to the poor.
- To fast on the prescribed occasions.
- To make at least one pilgrimage to *Mecca*.

HADITH: The Hadith are a collection of writings about things that *Muhammad* said or did. The Hadith reflect things that were passed along verbally until they were compiled about 200 years after Muhammad. Both the **Shiites** and **Sunnis** often disagree on what the Hadith consists of because each rejects reports of comments or actions that would have to be sourced by someone in the other denomination. The Hadith (things Muhammad said or did), along with the **Qur'an** (things **Allah** said or did, according to Muhammad), was and is heavily used and influential in the development of each **Islamic** denomination's interpretation and application of **Sharia** Law.

It is true that some of the Hadith tells stories of how Muhammad lied to gain the trust of his enemies, only to turn on them and kill them later. These stories are not always treated with the same emphasis among denominations or by various Islamic religious leaders. The everyday **Muslim** might not even view these as primary to their sense of how to live for Allah. It is important to realize the stories exist and are important, but also that there is no single standard to which they are treated across the board for Muslims. In *some* ways this is no different than differing views in the **Christian** world. Lying is considered ungodly across the board in the Christian world; however, there are other issues on which various Christian denominations differ: the place of women in Christian leadership positions; purpose and methods of baptism; communion; etc.

HAGAR: Egyptian maidservant to Sarah, **Abraham's** wife. Hagar was the mother of **Ishmael**. Because Sarah was barren and couldn't have a child, Sarah had Abraham sleep with Hagar in an attempt to fulfill one of God's **promises** to Abraham, and because Sarah really wanted a child. Having a man sleep with a wife's maidservant in order to have a child was culturally acceptable in their day when the wife could not conceive. Another cultural custom was that when a man did sleep with a maidservant, he was responsible to care for and protect both the mother and any offspring they had. God had Abraham go against this cultural custom and promised Hagar that Ishmael would be blessed with many descendants, which he was. **Muhammad** said that Ishmael was the actual first born of Abraham and was the father of the **Muslim** line.

Appendix 2: Definitions

HAMAS: Literally, "Enthusiasm." Hamas is a *Sunni* Islamic political group founded in 1987 to liberate *Palestine* from *Israeli* occupation and to re-establish an *Islamic* state there. Hamas has governed the Gaza Strip since 2007 when it won the majority in the Palestinian Parliament. Hamas also has a military arm, which has attacked both military and civilian targets in recent years, including suicide bombings. Peace agreements and armed conflict with Israel continue to come and go, depending on the political activities of Israel, Hamas and Israel's *Muslim* neighboring states.

HEZBOLLAH: Literally, "Party of God (*Allah*)." Hezbollah is a *Shiite* militant and political group, originally based in Lebanon. Many Western governments classify Hezbollah as primarily a terrorist organization, although it has grown to the point of having seats in the Lebanese government. Hezbollah was originally founded with the goal of removing *Israel* from Lebanon. In 2000, Israel had fully withdrawn from southern Lebanon, and Hezbollah modified its goals to removing Israel from all lands it occupies. Hezbollah has often received military training and aid from Iran. It has received political support from the Shiite government in Syria. When the majority *Sunni* population in Syria began a pro-democracy movement in 2011, Hezbollah sent 4,000 Iranian-trained fighters into Syria to support the Shiite-led government.

IMAM: A leader of *Muslim* worship.

ISAAC: Son of *Abraham* and Sarah. His half-brother was *Ishmael*, whose mother was *Hagar*. The *Bible* indicates God passed His three promises from Abraham to Isaac. Isaac had two sons, *Esau* and *Jacob* (Genesis 25:24-26).

The *Qur'an* (37:112-113) indicates that Isaac was born second, after Ishmael, and that he too was righteous, was a prophet (see *Prophet, Muslim View of*), and was blessed by *Allah*; but, the proper lineage passed through Ishmael.

ISHMAEL: Literally "God will hear." Son of **Abraham** and **Hagar**, Sarah's maidservant (Genesis 16:1-2, 15-16). Hagar was eventually kicked out of Abraham's home, but God promised to bless Ishmael, giving him many descendants. (Genesis 16:10-12).

Muhammad traced his linage to Abraham through Ishmael. The *Qur'an* (37:102-112) indicates that Ishmael is the firstborn, before *Isaac*, and as such would be the son to continue God's three *promises*. The Qur'an also indicates that Abraham later went to see Ishmael in what is now *Mecca*. It says that, in Mecca, Abraham and Ishmael built an altar and worshipped God. Today the site of that altar is a temple called, "*Ka'ba*." This is a holy site for *Muslims*.

ISIS (ISIL): *Islamic* State of Iraq and Syria (translated), also known as ISIL (Islamic State of Iraq and Levant). The Levant is a region in the Middle East that refers to the lands of Cyprus, *Israel*, Jordan, Lebanon, Syria, *Palestine* and a portion of southern Turkey. As of 2014, ISIS is an unrecognized *Muslim* state formed by a militant *jihadist* group by the same name. The goal of this Muslim group is to claim and unite Iraq and the Levant under a *Sunni* Caliphate (see also *Caliph*). ISIS is not tolerant of *Shiite* Muslims or *Christians*. In its beginnings, ISIS had close ties with *Al-Qaeda*, but as of 2014 functions independently of Al-Qaeda.

ISLAM: Literally "submission." The religious faith whose adherents view *Muhammad* as the Last Prophet, who accept the *Qur'an* as the sacred record of *Allah's* (God's) revelations to Muhammad, and who adhere to the *Five Pillars of Faith*. There are two major denominations (or sects) of Islam: *Shiite* and *Sunni*. However, other smaller denominations exist within those two. At times, any of the separate denominations might turn hostile towards the others.

ISRAEL (ISRAELITES): Literally, "He contends with God." Israel is the name God eventually gave *Jacob*; it is also the name of the *Jewish* nation or people. The nation of Israel traces its lineage

Appendix 2: Definitions

through Jacob and then *Isaac* to *Abraham*. Jacob's twelve sons' descendants become known as the Twelve Tribes of Israel (Genesis 49:1-28). They are also called, "Israelites."

JACOB: Literally, "He who takes by the heel." Jacob is the second son of *Isaac* and is the brother of *Esau*. Jacob deceptively acquired the birthright from his older brother, Esau. God later renamed Jacob, "*Israel*," (Genesis 35:9-10). Jacob had 12 sons, who would later father the "Twelve Tribes of Israel. It is through Jacob that the *Jewish* linage is identified (Exodus 3:15).

JERUSALEM: The most holy city for those of the *Jewish* faith. This is the city where the Jewish Temple was originally built and where it must be rebuilt in the future. It is only in this temple that sacrifices required under the Jewish Law may be offered. The last Temple was destroyed in 70 A. D. by the Roman general *Titus*.

Jerusalem is the third most holy city for those of the faith of *Islam*. It was from this city that *Muhammad* ascended, in a vision, into the presence of *Allah*. The last place he touched on the earth is viewed as sacred. The Dome of the Rock, a mosque in Jerusalem, is built on that sacred site. This mosque is located on the ruins of the ancient Jewish Temple.

JESUS: see, **MESSAGE OF CHRIST**

JEW, JEWISH: see *Judaism*.

JIHAD: This term relates to the struggle of submitting to *Allah* and living as He would have one to live. There are many meanings attached to the concept of jihad, and different *Muslim* denominations and scholars interpret jihad in a variety of way. This is one of the confusing aspects of *Islam* for non-Muslims.

One interpretation is that jihad is a holy war of Islam against unbelievers, the enemies of Islam. To Muslims holding this interpretation, the holy war concept often involves primarily an external defense of Islam and the practice of their view of God's will, which is then expressed as justification for hostilities, manipulations, lying or terrorism against non-Muslims (including toward Muslims that are not of the same denomination). Those who are considered Muslim terrorists or extremists usually see jihad almost solely according to this interpretation.

A second aspect of jihad is as an internal or "spiritual" war against good and evil within one's self. This aspect of jihad involves the striving to be righteous according to one's interpretation of the ***Qur'an***, which can sometimes include the previous interpretation too!

JONAH: Often called, "The Reluctant Prophet." Jonah reflected the ***Jewish*** view that God made ***Israel*** the favored nation, and that everyone else is secondary. God made it very clear to Jonah that He cares for all peoples, even those who sin against Him. God's compassion and love for all is demonstrated in Jonah's situation. God called on Jonah to relate some warnings to the Assyrian capital city of Nineveh, in hopes the people there would turn to God. Jonah reluctantly cooperated, and was very upset when God spared Nineveh in response to their change of heart. Jonah is one of the several examples we examined to see how important it is to ***discern*** not only what God wants of us in a trial, but how God is trying to change and grow us personally.

JUDAISM: The religious faith whose adherents view themselves as the legitimate descendants of ***Abraham***, ***Isaac***, and ***Jacob***. The ***Tanakh*** are the divine authority for religious belief and observance. As of 2014, the majority of the peoples of Jewish descent do not adhere to the tenants of Judaism.

KA'BA: The temple of ***Abraham*** and ***Ishmael*** in ***Mecca*** that was cleansed and rededicated by ***Muhammad***. According to ***Islam***, the Ka'ba is where Abraham and Ishmael made a sacrifice to ***Allah*** (***Qur'an*** 2:127, 22:25-27). It is the center of the world for the faith of Islam.

KURDS: The Kurds are a unique ethnic group (culture, language, and religion) in the Middle East, mostly inhabiting a region known as Kurdistan. This region includes portions of Iran, Iraq, Syria, and

Appendix 2: Definitions

Turkey (most Kurds live in Turkey). Kurdish history dates back to 2400 B.C., when they occupied the same region as today. This gives them one of the longest ethnic histories in the Middle East. Although Kurds embraced the teaching of *Islam*, as a result of an Islamic military invasion around 700 A.D., their culture remained distinctly different from other *Muslims*. This early difference has consistently precipitated problems with other Muslims seeking to rule the Kurds. Kurds are mostly *Sunnis*. The Kurds have been seeking autonomy for Kurdistan from the various nations that governed the region since World War I.

LAW, THE JEWISH LAW: The *Jews*, the *Christians* and the *Muslims* each hold to certain *Divine Laws*. The Jewish Law is found in the *Torah* or Pentateuch (the first five books of the Old Testament); specifically it is found in Exodus, Leviticus, Numbers, and Deuteronomy. The Law consists of commandments, decrees, laws, judgments, guidelines, etc. that God gave to Moses for the Children of *Israel*. The purpose of the Law was to guide the internal and external lives of God's people, individually and collectively. The Law is intended to affect every aspect of an individual's life so that the individual's life would be God-honoring (Exodus 19:1-9; 20:1-26). The Law is part of the *Tanakh*.

MECCA: The city in Saudi Arabia where the *Ka'Ba* is located. It is the most sacred city in *Islam*. It was in this city where *Muhammad* first received a revelation from *Allah*. Only *Muslims* are allowed in this sacred city.

MEDINA: The second most sacred city in *Islam*. It is located in Saudi Arabia. The citizens of this city granted refuge to *Muhammad* when he was forced to flee from *Mecca* due to persecution regarding his teachings. The citizens of Medina accepted the teachings of Muhammad and assisted him in raising an army to "liberate" Mecca and to cleanse the *Ka'Ba*. Muhammad is buried in Medina.

MESSAGE OF CHRIST: The *Jews*, the *Christians* and the *Muslims* each hold to certain *Divine Laws*. Christians believe that Jesus was the promised Jewish Messiah and He fulfilled The Jewish ***Law*** (Matthew 5:17) given to the ***Israelites*** by God through Moses (Leviticus 26:46). Christians believe that Jesus was the Son of the God of Abraham, Isaac and Jacob (John 3:16). Christians believe Jesus was the fulfillment of the Old Testament (Jewish) Law in that He lived the perfect life.

The sacrifice of Jesus on the cross was an act of love which made it possible for each member of humanity to enter into a loving, personal, transformational relationship with God, which involves this life as well as the eternal life. Jesus' teachings and commands are applicable to anyone who enters into a relationship with God through Jesus Christ. Jesus' teachings and commands center on love, peace and sacrifice. Jesus often indicated that ***discernment***, self-examination and introspection were important to applying His teachings to real-life (Mathew 7:5; 13:9, 15-16, 43; 15:15-16; 16:3; Mark 8:17-18; Luke 10:23-24; 14:35). This theme of discernment is echoed in Proverbs 1:2; 2:3, 5, 9; 10:13; 14:27; 28:7; Isaiah 27:11; 1 Corinthians 2:12-13, 11:28; 2 Corinthians 13:5; Philippians 1:9; 1 Thessalonians 5:21-22; 2 Timothy 4:3-4; Hebrews 5:14.

Followers of Jesus Christ, since He fulfilled the Jewish Law, are obliged to follow the higher "Law of loving God and our neighbor" (Matthew 22:36-40) as prescribed by the Lord (see also 1 John 3:18-24). This "Law" can lead to humility, selflessness, sacrifice, service, and inner peace, when we let God live it through us. The focus of this "Law" is that we discern the guidance of the Holy Spirit, which shows us how to let God live it through us. Discerning the guidance of the Holy Spirit involves looking at the heart and letting God change what is in it.

MUHAMMAD (570 A.D. – 632 A.D.): Considered by ***Muslims*** to be the last and final ***prophet*** of God (see ***Prophet, Muslim View of***). Muhammad traces his linage to ***Abraham*** through ***Ishmael***. He was 40 years old when he received the revelations for the ***Qur'an***. The recording of the revelations was completed in about 656 A.D. Muhammad converted the Saudi peninsula to ***Islam*** by the sword. He lived to be about 62 years old.

Appendix 2: Definitions

MUSLIM: An individual who holds to the faith of *Islam*.

MUSLIM BROTHERHOOD: A transnational *Sunni*, *Islamic* political organization founded in Egypt in 1928. It started by preaching Islam, teaching the literate and establishing hospitals. As it grew, its goal to make the *Qur'an* and Sunni beliefs the sole reference for the *Muslim* life at the individual, family, and state levels took on violent expressions. After World War II, it had more than 2 million members. It is known for politically motivated violence and for the beginnings of *Hamas*. The Muslim Brotherhood has often been banned or repressed in Muslim countries, as the organization has been known to use political violence. Even with these setbacks, the Muslim Brotherhood still continues to win powerful support among Sunni Muslims, including powerful political and financial support.

PALESTINE: The land of *Israel* became known as Palestine after the third *Jewish* revolt against the Romans, the first of which was crushed in 70 A.D. (see page 46). Palestine can refer to all or part of the land between the Mediterranean Sea and the Jordan River, as well as to the former country of Israel. The geography of Palestinian lands typically covers at least part, if not the whole, of the Promised Land. The boundaries of Palestine have changed through the years based on who controlled it. At the end of the 1940's, Palestine was ruled by the British. After World War II and with British support, the United Nations passed a resolution partitioning Palestine into a part Jewish and part Arab state. This led to a civil war, and the state of Israel emerged in 1948. Over half a million Palestinians fled or were driven out following the civil war. While the boundaries of today's Palestinian state are relatively stable, they have been known to change as a result of the wars and conflicts between Israel, various *Islamic* movements, and Israel's neighboring *Muslim* countries.

PROMISES, GOD'S THREE: (see also page 8) God made three promises to *Abraham* around 2000 B.C. These are recorded in Genesis 12.

1. Personal blessing: "I will make you a great Nation." (Genesis 12:2)
2. Universal blessing: "In you, all families...will be blessed." (Genesis 12:3)
3. National blessing: "To your descendants I will give this land." (Genesis 12:1, 7) The boundaries of the Promised Land are outlined in Genesis 15:18-21; Numbers 34:1-2; Ezekiel 47:13-23.

The Jewish view of these promises is found on page 36. The Christian view of these promises is found on page 44. The Muslim view of these promises is found on page 52.

Muslims do not see the ***Jews*** or ***Christians*** as being able to claim the fulfillment of God's promises to Abraham. The Muslims see the Jews as being a very resistant people toward God. Muslims believe this is why the Jews have been enslaved or scattered throughout the world for so much of their history. The Muslims see Christians as being too materialistic. This is why Muslims believe that the God of Abraham, ***Isaac*** and ***Jacob*** does not favor the Jews or the Christians. This is why Muslims believe the God of Abraham provided the ***Qur'an***, the "Final Testament," to ***Muhammad***, the last prophet.

PROPHETS, THE: see ***Tanakh***.

PROPHETS, MUSLIM VIEW OF BIBLICAL: The ***Qur'an*** speaks of many individuals mentioned in the ***Tanakh*** and the Christian ***Bible***. However, ***Muslims*** do not see some of these individuals in the same light a ***Christian*** or a ***Jew*** might. The following (the list is not all inclusive) are seen in ***Islam*** as important prophets of their time; however, ***Jesus*** is not seen as God's Son, the Messiah:
- Adam (first prophet)
- ***Abraham***
- ***Ishmael***
- Moses
- Jesus
- ***Muhammad*** (last prophet)

Appendix 2: Definitions

QUR'AN: (see also page 7) Literally "reciting." This is the sacred Book of the faith of *Islam*. These writings are the revelations received by *Muhammad* from *Allah*. They represent ultimate truth and will not be replaced.

SEMITE (SEMETIC): This term is often mistaken to mean a reference strictly to *Jews*. In actuality it refers to a person who descended from Shem, the second son of Noah. The Jews, Arabs, Assyrians, Phoenicians, and Babylonians are all considered Semites, or descendants of Noah's son Shem.

SHARIA LAW: Literally "Law." The *Jews*, the *Christians* and the *Muslims* each hold to certain *Divine Laws*. Sharia is the moral and religious code of the faith of *Islam*. As with many systems of law, there are some varied interpretations of it; however, Sharia Law sharply differs from typical laws in "modern" countries. The controversies around Sharia have often resulted in violence by its advocates. Sharia Law is based on the *Qur'an*, the *Hadith*, and the example of *Muhammad*. Many Islamic movements seek to have all Muslims to be governed under Sharia Law, as opposed to the laws of a country in which a Muslim might live. Where permitted, Islamic legal authorities will pass their rulings according to Sharia Law. Sharia Law is very controversial, as it is considered by many to be against human, women's, and minority's rights and freedoms.

SHIITE: Literally "Follower." Also translated as Shia or Shiah. A person of the Shiah denomination (sect) of *Islam*. Shiites believe that God has designated a spiritual "lineage" through the bloodline of *Muhammad*, which functions as the source of spiritual and secular guidance for the Islamic community. Adherents of Shia believe that *Ali ibn Abi Talib*, a cousin and son-in-law of Muhammad, was the legitimate successor of Muhammad. Therefore, this denomination (sect) of Islam rejects the first three *Caliphs* who succeeded Muhammad under the *Sunnis*. In 912 A.D. Muhammad's successor through Ali ibn Abi Talib was killed and his son, his successor, disappeared. Since, the Shiites have been waiting for the "Hidden Imam" to reappear. This is the 2nd largest Islamic denomination behind Sunnis.

SHIITE CONTROVERSY: The *Shiite* Controversy led to a split among Shiites. In 912 A.D., the *Imam* disappeared. Eventually, a person claiming to be the divine Imam appeared in 1017 A.D, but most Shiites rejected that Imam. The group of Shiites that accepted the particular Imam as the "Hidden Imam" are known today as the *Druze*.

SUNNI: Literally "custom, code of behavior." A person of the Sunna denomination (sect) of *Islam*. The denomination (sect) of Islam that holds that the *Qur'an* was to be interpreted by the teachings and practices of *Muhammad*. Sunnis acknowledge the first four *Caliphs* as the rightful successors of Muhammad. This is the largest denomination of Islam. Sunnis can elect their *Imams* and Caliphs. Again, *Shiites* do not elect Imams because Shiites believe the Imam must be in the direct bloodline of Muhammad.

TANAKH: see also page 7. This is the Hebrew "Bible." There are three major divisions that make up these *Jewish* sacred Scriptures. One division is the first five books known as the Torah, literally "*Law*." The Torah is also called, "The Books of Moses." A second division is the Prophets. The Prophets consist of the major (longer writings) and minor (smaller writings) of the prophets. A third division is called, "The Writings." The Writings consist of the historical and poetic writings that make up the balance of the Tanakh, for example, Psalms, Proverbs, Ecclesiastes, Song of Solomon, etc. These three divisions of the Tanakh are almost identical to the Christian *Bible's* Old Testament, yet they are arranged in a different order. Collectively, known as the Tanakh, the three divisions are very similar to the *Christian* Old Testament.

TITUS: This is not referring to the Titus of the Christian *Bible's* New Testament but to the Roman general who destroyed the temple in *Jerusalem* in 70 A.D. He later became the Roman Emperor.

TORAH: see *Tanakh*.

WRITINGS, THE: see *Tanakh*.

Appendix 2: Definitions

APPENDIX 3: REFERENCES

A Dictionary of Judaism and Christianity (1st Trinity Press edition). Philadelphia: Trinity Press International, 1991.

New American Standard Bible. Chicago: Moody Press, 1975.

The Holy Qur'an (13th edition). Rabwah, Pakistan: The Oriental and Religious Publishing Corporation, Ltd., 1982.

Bamberger, Bernard J. *The Story of Judaism.* New York: Schoken Books, 1964.

"Background Notes." www.state.gov. 2011. http://www.state.gov/r/pa/ei/bgn/

Braden, Charles S. *The World's Religions: A Short History.* Nashville: Abingdon, 1954.

Clark, Jr., William J. with CH (COL) William J. Clark, Ret. *Feelings 101: Pain to Peace, 2nd Edition.* Keys To Understanding Life Series, 2013.

Crim, Keith, editor. *Abingdon Dictionary of the Bible.* Nashville: Abingdon, 1981.

Donin, Rabbi Hayim Halevy. *To Be a Jew: A Guide to Jewish Observance in Contemporary Life.* New York: Basic Books, 1972.

Eastern Europe, Russia and Central Asia, Volume 4. Taylor and Francis Group, 2004, ISBN 9781857431872

Fackenheim, Emil L. *What is Judaism? An Interpretation for the Present Age.* New York: Summit Books, 1987.

Appendix 3: References

"Facts and Figures." www.saudiembassy.net. 24 May 2012. http://www.saudiembassy.net/about/country-information/facts_and_figures/ (The flag representing Sunnis in this book is an older version of the Saudi Arabian flag.)

"Flag of the Bahrain." www.wikipedia.org. 16 November 2009. http://en.wikipedia.org/wiki/File:Flag_of_Bahrain.svg (Shiah or Shiite flag) (Note: It seems that each country seems to use a different Shiite flag. Even some Shiite Imams have their own Shiite flags. The flag representing the Shiite religion in this book is actually the flag of Bahrain.)

"Flag of the Muslim League." www.wikipedia.org. 30 December 2007. http://en.wikipedia.org/wiki/File:Flag_of_Muslim_League.png (The flag representing the Muslim religion in this book is the Muslim League flag.)

Filkins, Dexter (September 30, 2013). "The Shadow Commander." *The New Yorker*.

Hahn, Ernest. *How to Respond to Muslims*. Concordia Publishing House. St. Louis, Missouri, 1995.

Hallett, Robin. *Africa Since 1875*. Ann Arbor, Michigan: The University of Michigan Press (1974), p. 138.

Herzog, Chaim. *The Arab-Israeli Wars*. New York: Vintage Books, 1984

Hinnelis, John R., editor. *The Facts on File Dictionary of Religions*. New York: Facts on File, 1984.

Hiro, Dilip. *Holy Wars: The Rise of Islamic Fundamentalism*. New York: Routledge, 1989.

McDowell, Josh. *Evidence That Demands a Verdict*. Campus Crusade for Christ, 1972.

Kendall, David. "Druze People." FOTW Flags Of The World website. 29 July 2011 http://www.fotw.net/flags/sy-druz.html (Druze flag)

Kennedy, Hugh. *The Great Arab Conquests*. Da Capo Press, Pennsylvania, 2007.

Lewis, Bernard. *Islam in History: Ideas, People, and Events in the Middle East*. Chicago: Open Court, 1993.

Mishory, Alec. "The Flag and the Emblem." Israel Ministry of Foreign Affairs. 28 April 2003 www.mfa.gov.il (Israel flag)

"Muqtada al-Sadr." 720mpreunion.org. 720th Military Police Battalion Reunion Association and History Project. 2003. http://720mpreunion.org/history/biography_historical/muqtada-al-sadr/muqtada-al-sadr.html (Sunni flag)

Nyrop, Richard F., editor. *Iran: A Country Study*. Washington, D.C.: The American University, 1978.

Nyrop, Richard F., editor. *Iraq: A Country Study*. Washington, D.C.: The American University, 1979.

Nyrop, Richard F. and others.. *Saudi Arabia: A Country Study*. Washington, D.C.: The American University, 1976.

Nyrop, Richard F., editor. *Syria: A Country Study*. Washington, D.C.: The American University, 1979.

Pipes, Daniel. *In the Path of God: Islam and Political Power*. New York: Basic Books, 1983.

Rutherford, Bruce. *Egypt After Mubarak*. Princeton: Princeton UP, 2008.

Schimel, Annemarie. *Islam: An Introduction*. Albany: State University of New York Press, 1992.

Appendix 3: References

Schoeps, Hans Joachim. *The Religions of Mankind*. Garden City, N. Y.: Doubleday, 1960.

Smart, Ninian. *The Religious Experience of Mankind*. New York: Scribner, 1984.

Smith, Huston. *The World's Religions*. San Francisco: Harper, 1991.

Tarbush, Muhammad. *Reflections of a Palestinian*. American-Arab Affairs Council, Washington, D.C., 1986

Unger, Merrill F. *Unger's Bible Dictionary*. 3rd ed. Chicago; Moody Press, 1967.

USA Today, 2007-09-24, "Tension between Sunnis, Shiites emerging in USA"

Wagner, William. *How Islam Plans to Change the World*. Kregel Publications, Grand Rapids, Michigan, 2004.

Williams, John A. *Islam*. New York: G. Braziller. 1961.

Williams, John A. *The Word of Islam*. Austin: University of Texas Press, 1994.

"Who are Hamas?" London: BBC News. January 26, 2006

Wright, Lawrence. *The Looming Tower: Al-Qaeda and the Road to 9/11*. Knopf. ISBN 0-375-41486-X. 2006

APPENDIX 4: LIST OF FIGURES

Figure 1.1 – Who Was Where at Time of God's Promises 11

Figure 1.2 – Abraham's House in Ur 12

Figure 1.3 – Biblical Descriptions of the Promised Land 13

Figure 1.4 – Abraham's Descendants at the Time of the Exodus 27

Figure 1.5 – Promised Land at the Time the of the Exodus 35

Figure 1.6 – Spread of Christianity c. 600 A.D. 50

Figure 1.7 – Spread of Islam c. 900 A.D. 56

Figure 1.8 - Timeline of the Religious Origins of the Middle East 57

Figure 1.9 – Map of Modern Day Middle East 64

OTHER TITLES IN THE *KEYS TO UNDERSTANDING LIFE SERIES*

www.Feelings101.com

Discusses the Bible's principles for discerning God's guidance in any trial we face.

A comprehensive self-paced course and resource for understanding how God designed us to experience and participate in spiritual battles.

Examines the Bible's *7 Spiritual Principles* for listening to the voice of God with the heart during trials.

www.Feelings102.com

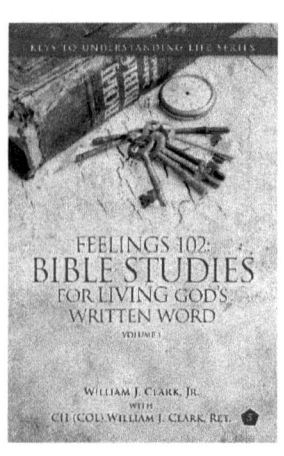

23 lessons in Biblical trials, designed to train Christians in dealing with trials.

Each lesson's read-ahead is very light; great for busy Christians too.

Practical and eye-opening for individuals, but dynamic and perfect for small groups of 3-10.

Facilitator is optional, not required. Facilitator info is provided in the book, with more on the *Keys* website.

For more titles, visit www.KeysToUnderstandingLife.org.

Religious Origins of the Middle East Crisis, 2nd Edition

ABOUT THE AUTHORS

The father and son team combine a variety of experiences including formal theological education, creating spiritually intimate fellowships and teaching powerful personal transformation skills possible in Christ. From their home in Texas, they help others learn how to enjoy the enriching and interactive life of being a disciple of Christ.

Learn more about the authors by visiting:
www.KeysToUnderstandingLife.org

www.ingramcontent.com/pod-product-compliance
Lightning Source LLC
Chambersburg PA
CBHW071706040426
42446CB00011B/1945